"The apostle Paul did not start 'movements.' He planted churches. We are overdue for a renewed emphasis on what the Bible emphasizes: prioritizing the church in missions. This excellent resource—written by two seasoned pastors serving in churches overseas—is just the antidote we need. Pastors, students, missionaries, mission committees, mission agencies, senders, and goers—everyone interested in missions will be helped by reading this book."
**Kevin DeYoung,** Senior Pastor, Christ Covenant Church, Matthews, North Carolina

"Far too much mission work today is gospel-less or gospel-light. Even more is church-less or church-light. This book—which is written not just for pastors and missionaries but for all of us—is biblically faithful, deeply needed, and extremely helpful. May God raise up thousands upon thousands of followers of Jesus who both love the church and live to see it multiplied among all the nations."
**David Platt,** Pastor, McLean Bible Church, McLean, Virginia; Founder, Radical

"In one sense the theme of this book is ordinary—the church is vital for missions. But in another sense it is extraordinary and explosive since so many have forgotten that message. Folmar and Logsdon show from the Scriptures that the church is vital for every aspect of missions, and they also provide many examples and stories to illustrate that truth. Pastors, missionaries, and church members need to hear the truth unfolded in this book. It will make an eternal difference."
**Thomas R. Schreiner,** James Buchanan Harrison Professor of New Testament Interpretation, The Southern Baptist Theological Seminary

"*Prioritizing the Church in Missions* should be required reading for missionaries and their churches. Written by two seasoned pastors, this book is grounded in biblical truth, enriched with practical application, and filled with both wise cautions and compelling examples from the mission field. The authors convincingly argue that bad ecclesiology weakens missions—harming missionaries and undermining the gospel—while a church-centered approach rightly establishes the church as both the means and the goal of missions. More than just a practical guide, this book offers a theologically rich and definitive vision for missions as God intended."

**Jenny Manley,** author, *The Good Portion—Christ: Delighting in the Doctrine of Christ*; podcast host

"I trust no one more to speak on the church and missions than John Folmar and Scott Logsdon. This book is a concise distillation of their convictions about the church as the God-ordained means to display his manifold wisdom and uphold the truth of the gospel as a pillar and buttress. It is also a plea for those convictions to be applied to the task of missions. They argue convincingly and winsomely that the church is both the means and aim of God's mission to make himself known and call his own to himself. I will be buying these by the case to pass out at my church, in my classroom, and beyond. Read, recalibrate, and rejoice in the wisdom of our God!"

**Matt Bennett,** Director of Long-Term Ministries, Reaching & Teaching International Ministries; Associate Professor of Missions and Theology, Cedarville University

"The church must be at the center of missions, as God's human agency for his saving work in the world. Written by authors with extensive experience, this book affirms vital biblical truths about the church and gives valuable advice about how to keep God's church central in God's mission. It is packed with ministry stories, historical examples, and practical illustrations to guide church leaders and all sincere believers in applying these truths within their own contexts."

**Brian A. DeVries,** Principal, Mukhanyo Theological College; Church Planting Pastor, Grace Reformed Church, Pretoria, South Africa; author, *You Will Be My Witnesses*

"This excellent book offers a needed critique of the weaknesses in contemporary missions methodology. But more than that, Folmar and Logsdon have put forward a compelling biblical vision of how the church is the origin, means, and goal of missions. When missions prioritizes the church, it is good for the long-term growth of the gospel. I highly recommend this book."

**Eugene Low,** Lead Pastor, Grace Baptist Church, Singapore

"*Prioritizing the Church in Missions* is a compelling, Scripture-based call to return to the biblical blueprint for reaching the nations. John Folmar and Scott Logsdon weave together Scripture, history, and their own frontline experiences to demonstrate why the local church isn't just a bystander in missions—it's the beating heart of it. This book challenges the pragmatism that has crept into modern missions, with methodologies focused on speed or quick results, and instead offers a vision that is both timeless and urgent: healthy churches planting healthy churches. It's a must-read for anyone serious about seeing the gospel flourish globally."

**Greg A. Dye,** Founder, Global Serve International

"Biblical missions work is always driven by and centered on the local church. In this book, John and Scott show us what church-centered missions looks like and how it best reflects God's plan for missions. The book is filled with personal stories, church history, and life-giving instruction. I look forward to using it to help frame our church's understanding for years to come."

**Jason Dees,** Senior Pastor, Christ Covenant, Atlanta, Georgia

"The last few decades have brought encouraging biblical revivals in counseling and ecclesiology. But what's still missing? A revival in missiology. This small book takes a huge first step toward that goal. The authors' insistence that the church is both the means and the end of missions provides the solid foundation we need to build a truly biblical missiology for the third millennium."

**Sam Masters,** missionary to Argentina; author, *Doing Missions*

"*Prioritizing the Church in Missions* is not just another way to do missions. It is the biblical way to go about the Great Commission. Folmar and Logsdon convincingly argue that sound theology (especially ecclesiology) needs to be the foundation of missions. Thus, the church needs to be the origin, means, and end of missions in order for missions to be and accomplish what God intends with it. This is a must-read for everyone involved in missions . . . and that should be every one of us if we know and follow Christ."

**Matthias Lohmann,** Pastor, Free Evangelical Church, Munich, Germany; Chairman, Evangelium21

"Drawing upon the Scriptures, John Folmar and Scott Logsdon wisely and winsomely explain why biblical missions is church-based through and through. Rich and readable. Constructive and corrective. Insightful and inviting. Clear and compelling. This spiritually oxygen-rich book should be on your reading list this week."

**David B. Garner,** President, The Southgate Fellowship; Charles Krahe Professor of Systematic Theology, Westminster Theological Seminary

"With a clear biblical philosophy for missions, inspiring true stories, and motivating, Christ-honoring exhortations, *Prioritizing the Church in Missions* equips pastors and local churches to engage in the Great Commission. At a time when Christians are pursuing misguided approaches to missions, seasoned missionaries Scott and John appeal to the Scriptures to reveal how God ordained *the church*, which includes your church, to be central in his plan for reaching the nations. This book will have a permanent place in my library and remain on my short list of giveaway resources."

**Bobby Scott,** Pastor of Discipleship, Community of Faith Bible Church, South Gate, California; Council Member, The Gospel Coalition

"This powerful and thought-provoking book beautifully reveals the centrality of the church in God's mission. The authors masterfully demonstrate that the church is not only the origin of mission work but also its means and ultimate goal, grounded in the very message of the Bible itself. What sets this book apart are the vivid real-life illustrations the authors bring from personal experience—stories that not only illuminate the truths shared but also make them deeply relatable and impactful. A must-read for anyone passionate about missions and the church's God-given purpose in the world!"

**Sherif A. Fahim,** New Testament Chair, Alexandria School of Theology, Egypt; General Director, El-Soora Ministries

"What's missing in missions? More workers? More resources? Greater access to hard places? While all of these are important, John Folmar and Scott Logsdon argue that the most critical missing element is a biblical emphasis on the local church. In this compelling book, they seek to restore the church to its rightful place as the origin, means, and goal of missions. With careful biblical support, personal stories, and historical insight, they critique modern missions movements—not through caricature but with clarity and conviction—while offering a positive, church-centered way forward. This is an invaluable resource for church members, pastors, missionaries, and mission agencies seeking to think more biblically and ecclesiologically about missions to the glory of God."

**Omar Johnson,** Pastor, Temple Hills Baptist Church, Marlow Heights, Maryland

"Evangelicals agree that Jesus commissioned us to reach the nations, but we often differ on how missions should be carried out. In *Prioritizing the Church in Missions*, John Folmar and Scott Logsdon argue that missions must be church-centered, with local churches as both the means and the goal of gospel work. Pushing back against pragmatic and movement-driven models, they make a compelling case that Christ builds his church through biblical preaching, discipleship, and local church cooperation. If you want a theologically grounded and practical vision for missions that prioritizes the local church, this book is an essential read."

**Juan R. Sanchez,** Senior Pastor, High Pointe Baptist Church, Austin, Texas; author, *Seven Dangers Facing Your Church*

# PRIORITIZING THE CHURCH
## IN MISSIONS

**9Marks Church-Centered Missions**

Edited by Jonathan Leeman, Brooks Buser, and Scott Logsdon

*Prioritizing the Church in Missions*, by John Folmar and Scott Logsdon

*Prioritizing Missions in the Church*, by Aaron Menikoff and Harshit Singh

# PRIORITIZING THE CHURCH IN MISSIONS

John Folmar and
Scott Logsdon

Foreword by Conrad Mbewe

WHEATON, ILLINOIS

*Prioritizing the Church in Missions*

© 2025 by John Folmar and Scott Logsdon

Published by Crossway
   1300 Crescent Street
   Wheaton, Illinois 60187

All rights reserved. No part of this publication may be reproduced, stored in a retrieval system, or transmitted in any form by any means, electronic, mechanical, photocopy, recording, or otherwise, without the prior permission of the publisher, except as provided for by USA copyright law. Crossway® is a registered trademark in the United States of America.

Cover design: Jordan Singer

First printing 2025

Printed in the United States of America

Scripture quotations are from the ESV® Bible (The Holy Bible, English Standard Version®), © 2001 by Crossway, a publishing ministry of Good News Publishers. Used by permission. All rights reserved. The ESV text may not be quoted in any publication made available to the public by a Creative Commons license. The ESV may not be translated in whole or in part into any other language.

All emphases in Scripture quotations have been added by the authors.

Trade paperback ISBN: 979-8-8749-0230-8
ePub ISBN: 979-8-8749-0232-2
PDF ISBN: 979-8-8749-0231-5

---

**Library of Congress Cataloging-in-Publication Data**

Names: Folmar, John, 1966– author. | Logsdon, Scott, 1971– author.
Title: Prioritizing the church in missions / John Folmar and Scott Logsdon.
Description: Wheaton, Illinois : Crossway, 2025. | Series: 9Marks church-centered missions | Includes bibliographical references and index.
Identifiers: LCCN 2024045080 (print) | LCCN 2024045081 (ebook) | ISBN 9798874902308 (trade paperback) | ISBN 9798874902315 (pdf) | ISBN 9798874902322 (epub)
Subjects: LCSH: Missions. | Missions—Biblical teaching.
Classification: LCC BV2061.3 .F65 2025 (print) | LCC BV2061.3 (ebook) | DDC 266—dc23/eng/20250219
LC record available at https://lccn.loc.gov/2024045080
LC ebook record available at https://lccn.loc.gov/2024045081

---

Crossway is a publishing ministry of Good News Publishers.

| VP | | 34 | 33 | 32 | 31 | 30 | 29 | 28 | 27 | 26 | 25 |
|----|----|----|----|----|----|----|----|----|----|----|----|
| 15 | 14 | 13 | 12 | 11 | 10 | 9 | 8 | 7 | 6 | 5 | 4 | 3 | 2 | 1 |

*To our missions-minded wives,*
*our fellow heirs in the greatest cause.*

# Contents

Series Preface *ix*

Foreword by Conrad Mbewe *xv*

Introduction: The Launchpad and Outcome of Missions *1*

1 What Is the Church? *21*

2 What Is Missions? *57*

3 Church as the Origin of Missions *85*

4 Church as the Means of Missions *115*

5 Church as the Goal of Missions *139*

6 Churches Cooperating for Missions *165*

Conclusion *187*

General Index *191*

Scripture Index *201*

# Series Preface

Church-centered missions depends on four principles.

1. *Christianity is church shaped.* The gospel does not only promise God's mercy and forgiveness to individuals; it also makes us a people (Eph. 2:11–22; 1 Pet. 2:10). Conversion signs us up for a family photograph. It makes us a "we," and the local church is where we embody and live out the "we." As such, the Christian life is a church member's life. Following Jesus as disciples means doing so in the fellowship of the church. This principle is the foundation for the next two.

2. *Churches are the means and ends of missions.* If plank one is true, then our view of missions should also be church shaped. Among other things, that means the most important missionary training doesn't occur in seminary or at a missions agency training center. It

occurs in the years a Christian spends being a member of a healthy church. Who is the Great Commission for? Not just individual Christians, but churches. Movements are not the biblically ordained missionary method. Nor are unaccountable individuals. Nor are missions agencies. Churches are the Bible's missionary method. They are the staging areas for missions. Missions happens when churches send elders, deacons, and members to plant churches, both locally and internationally. Missions is church planting across significant barriers, which are usually geographic, cultural, or linguistic.

3. *Missions works best when churches work together.* The churches of the New Testament pursued church planting across barriers—missions—by working together. The churches in Antioch and Jerusalem worked together in support of Paul and Barnabas (Acts 11; 13; 15). The church in Derbe sent Paul and Barnabas back to Lystra, Iconium, and Antioch to appoint elders (14:21–23). Paul sent good preachers from one church to another (2 Cor. 8:18). John told a church to receive and send faithful missionaries (3 John 5–8). He also condemned one church leader who tried to "go it alone"(3 John 9–10). Churches should always

aspire to cooperate. Two American or two Korean churches cooperate to send a missionary; or an American/Korean and international church cooperate to send a planter; or an American/Korean, international, and national-indigenous church partner to do the same. Agencies, when involved, facilitate; they're aids, not ecclesial authorities. Ecclesial authority belongs to each church working in partnership with others.

4. *Missions is Bible led.* The Bible is our best and only authoritative manual for the basics of missions. Missions work should therefore be biblically led, shaped, and directed. Scripture doesn't speak to all the methods a missionary might employ from context to context (working through an international church? working through an agency?). Nor does it address all the forms a new church might adopt (long or short sermons? Sunday school classes?). Yet it clearly establishes the necessary elements that make a church, no matter what the context. And it establishes the ordinary means of grace for our ministry (evangelizing, preaching, praying, singing, gathering, ordinances).

In light of these four principles, we define *missions* as church planting across significant barriers. To fill that out

## SERIES PREFACE

just a bit, missions involves churches sending qualified workers across linguistic, geographic, or cultural barriers to start or strengthen churches, especially in places where Christ has not been named.

Neither this definition nor the 9Marks Church-Centered Missions series covers every topic that's important for missions. And the authors in this series may not agree on every jot and tittle when it comes to the many debates among missionaries such as what kind of priority should be given to the unreached. Should we have emphasized those with no access to the gospel in our definition? The authors across this series might not agree with each other. Still, we do agree on the basic paradigm offered in these four principles. Therefore, we have sought to write these books somewhat together, with authors using common, agreed-upon language for defining the church-centered missions paradigm. We're attempting to offer a team vision, not just the solo perspectives of the individual authors involved.

We have also sought to involve both sending pastors and missionaries in writing nearly every volume. That's because our primary audience is the churches sending missionaries (pastors, missions committees, general members). Our secondary audience is the missionaries who are sent.

These short volumes don't say everything that needs to be said about missions. Still, we pray the series as a whole will

## SERIES PREFACE

help churches and missionaries everywhere recover a vision for the central role local churches should play in fulfilling the Great Commission.

*Jonathan Leeman with Brooks Buser and Scott Logsdon*

# Foreword

When God raised up William Carey and Adoniram Judson as pioneer missionaries toward the end of the eighteenth century, their testimonies stung the consciences of Christians in the Western world. Almost overnight, mission societies were born on both sides of the Atlantic, and thousands of missionaries were sent to places like South America, Africa, Asia, and beyond. The golden era of world missions was born!

Meanwhile, *churches* in the West were dying. Higher criticism and the scientific revolution tempted Christians to question their passed-down beliefs. Churches were changing their assumptions about the Bible and the miraculous. Bible colleges and seminaries, once full of young people preparing for gospel ministry, taught people to doubt the authenticity of the Bible and the exclusivity of the gospel. Despite magnificent buildings and majestic pipe organs, faith wilted in pulpits and then in the pews.

## FOREWORD

Many resisted these sad changes, but starting new churches wasn't the first thought on their minds. Instead, they channeled their energies and their money through *parachurch* organizations: the Baptist Missionary Society (1792), the London Missionary Society (1795), the Church Missionary Society (1799), the American Board of Commissioners for Foreign Missions (1810), the YMCA (1844), the YWCA (1855), the Student Volunteer Movement (1886), and the China Inland Mission (1865).

Almost none of the missionary societies born in the golden era of missions were church-based. Christians acknowledged that missions was the work of the church in some generic sense. And most early missionaries intended to plant congregations. Yet far more attention went to individual Christians. *They* should support the work of missions by giving and by going. There was little talk about how *churches* should raise up, send out, and support missionaries on the field. Instead, Christians began to regard agencies as the necessary means.

By the dawn of the twentieth century, the fight for the Bible had been largely won. "Bible churches" were established all over the Western world. And yet, parachurch organizations—not churches—still sent out the majority of our missionaries. It was the norm; only a few voices questioned it.

At the same time, individuals who had never served on the mission field and who were not qualified for leadership in

## FOREWORD

the church were now running Bible colleges, seminaries, and agencies; they were training future missionaries. The church looked on. They were the "go-to people" when someone needed to consult the experts about missions. Unfortunately, their expertise was theologically anemic and mostly relied on models borrowed from the business world. Using these methods, you could be successful on the mission field with little reliance on the Holy Spirit and no reference to the church! And many were "successful." They produced disciples after their own kind— lone-ranger Christians who didn't prioritize the bride of Christ.

Thankfully, by the beginning of this century, churches have started to wake up to the fact that they are not just supporting actors in the drama of missions. They are central players. Missions should be at the top of every church's agenda. This awakening has accompanied missionaries being alerted to the fact that so little missions work leads to healthy churches.

This book is a voice calling your church back to church-centered missions. The study of missions must start with the study of the church because missionaries must be nurtured in and sent out by churches. The primary work of missionaries should be establishing and supporting churches. All other work should revolve around that. Christians should channel the bulk of their support for missions through their local churches. Missionaries should remember that they are accountable to

## FOREWORD

their sending churches and not only to their agency bosses. This book calls churches to work together to achieve clear partnerships between church, agency, and missionary.

The authors are pastors of international, English-speaking churches in Muslim countries. Church life and missions work are the very air they breathe. They have studied this subject like surgeons in operating theaters, not as students taking online classes in the comfort of their own homes. They bring to the table theological depth, historical insight, and practical wisdom born from many years of experience. They are not throwing away the baby with the dirty bathwater. In fact, one of them worked for a missions agency for decades. And yet they still insist that the church must be prioritized from beginning to end.

These men call us to join them in doing what is right and biblical. Let's go along with them on this journey. Let's renew our vision of the preeminence of the church in missions. Let's see what our role should be in this great enterprise, even as ordinary Christians. Let's take our place to spread the fame of Christ through his bride. When we put the church in its rightful place in the work of missions, it will lead to the joy of all peoples and the glory of God.

*Conrad Mbewe*

PASTOR, KABWATA BAPTIST CHURCH, LUSAKA, ZAMBIA
FOUNDING CHANCELLOR, AFRICAN CHRISTIAN UNIVERSITY

Introduction

# The Launchpad and Outcome of Missions

In 2003 a church in California sent missionaries to an unreached tribe in Papua New Guinea. Within nine years the missionaries learned the tribe's language and culture. They experienced jungle living. They learned how to throw spears, hunt pigs, set up solar panels, and build an airfield. They also developed an alphabet for illiterate people, taught locals to read, and then translated God's word into their language. Many tribespeople, reading the Bible for the first time, responded to the gospel and were saved.

Yet the missionaries knew their job was not done.

One remarked, "Our work wasn't just about translating the Bible, much less about promoting literacy or building airstrips

### INTRODUCTION

or teaching the people about medicine. It was about leaving behind a church that was built on the Bible."[1] Only once an indigenous biblical church formed, complete with local leadership, did the missionaries feel like their work was done.

On one occasion, the missionaries and tribespeople celebrated the completion of the Bible into the Yembiyembi language. The tribespeople insisted that representatives from the missionaries' church be present to hand over the Bible to them. In their words, the Bible and the Christian faith had moved "from the mama church to a daughter church."[2]

Their phrase takes us to the very heart of what we believe missions is: churches sending qualified workers across linguistic, geographic, or cultural barriers to start or strengthen churches, especially in places where Christ has not been named.

Too often, the Western missionary enterprise overlooks the role of the church as both the means and end of missions. Yet if we were to ask Jesus, what would he say about the relationship between missions and the church?

For starters, he would remind us of his promise: "I will build my church" (Matt. 16:18). Then he would remind us how missions is the way to build his church: "This gospel of the kingdom

[1] *YembiYembi Unto the Nations*, YouTube, 30 min., 37 sec., December 16, 2016, Radius International, https://www.youtube.com/.

[2] *Yembi Unto the Nations*.

INTRODUCTION

will be proclaimed throughout the whole world as a testimony to all nations, and then the end will come" (Matt. 24:14).

Since Jesus's day, wherever the gospel of the kingdom has advanced, churches have formed. The process began in Jerusalem. The apostles preached the gospel, and "the Lord added to their number day by day those who were being saved" (Acts 2:47). Added to what number? The church in Jerusalem.

The story continues through the book of Acts. People preach. Churches form. Those churches send out others to preach, and more churches form. After persecution hit the church in Jerusalem, for instance, the saints "were all scattered throughout the regions of Judea and Samaria" and "those who were scattered went about preaching the word" (8:1, 4). A chapter later, Luke provides an update: "So the church throughout all Judea and Galilee and Samaria had peace and was being built up. And walking in the fear of the Lord and in the comfort of the Holy Spirit, it multiplied" (9:31).

It's a beautiful word—*multiplied*.

This process repeated in Antioch, Lystra, Iconium, Pisidian Antioch, Syria and Cilicia, Corinth, Caesarea, Troas, and Ephesus.[3] Churches are both the *outcome* of gospel preaching and the *platform* for more gospel preaching.

---

3   Acts 5:12; 11:26; 14:21; 15:41; 18:8, 22; 19:9; 20:6, 17.

## INTRODUCTION

Consider William Carey. Seven years after arriving in India, the father of modern missions moved with a team to Serampore in 1800. There, one biographer says, "They formed themselves into a church, with Carey as pastor, Marshman and Ward the deacons."[4] They preached and observed the ordinances, sang biblical songs, and encouraged one another's faith. "According to one eye-witness," the biographer continues, " '[Carey] stomped his foot vigorously to set the time' during the reglar worship services on Sunday."[5] Hindus and Muslims attended the gatherings out of curiosity. This congregation became the launchpad for missions into India.

Almost a century later, Samuel Zwemer established the Arabian Mission with "stations" at Basrah, Iraq; Muscat, Oman; and the island of Bahrain. At each station, churches were established in Arabic and English, initially meeting in rented houses. In those days, says one historian, "Sunday services, with the sounds of music and singing, were considered an evangelistic tool."[6] Zwemer believed the church was central to God's purposes among unreached peoples.

---

4 Timothy George, *Faithful Witness: The Life and Mission of William Carey* (Worcester, PA: Christian History Institute, 1998), 125.

5 George, *Faithful Witness*, 128.

6 Lewis R. Scudder III, *The Arabian Mission's Story: In Search of Abraham's Other Son* (Grand Rapids, MI: Eerdmans, 1995), 196.

INTRODUCTION

In 1902 Zwemer's wife, Amy, wrote of the "plain and simple" worship in Bahrain where "a few isolated believers meet to worship the God of Abraham and where we expect the blessing promised to Abraham that 'Ishmael shall live before me.'"[7] Inquirers were welcome. One eyewitness observed, "People are willing to stand outside looking in at the doorways and windows."[8] Decades later in Kuwait a pastor would urge his congregation "to sing louder so that it might be heard outside as clearly as was the voice of the *mu'azzin* (mosque prayer caller) across the street."[9]

These missionaries were not a special class of Christians who lived independently of churches. They were first and foremost members of a local congregation. They recognized that churches were both the *outcome* of the gospel and the *platform* for the gospel to go forward and start more churches.

In Scripture and throughout history, churches have been central to the missions enterprise. Neither movements nor parachurch agencies nor unaccountable individuals are the God-ordained method—churches are. Indeed, they are:

7   Alfred Mason and Frederick Barney, *History of the Arabian Mission* (New York: The Board of Foreign Missions Reformed Church in America, 1926), 126–27.

8   Mason and Barney, *History of the Arabian Mission*, 127.

9   Scudder, *Arabian Mission's Story*, 196.

5

INTRODUCTION

- *the origin of missions*, equipping, training, and sending missionaries into the harvest;
- *the means of missions*, functioning as Jesus's discipleship program for new believers everywhere; and
- *the end of missions*, since local congregations serve as the focal point of God's glory on earth.

We can summarize this by saying *churches are the means and ends of missions*. This phrase provides one of the foundational planks in the church-centered missions paradigm.

## Our Doctrine of Salvation and the Church

Why are the church and missions so intertwined? Because the gospel makes us church members. The church is part and parcel of our very doctrine of salvation. Listen to Peter, and notice the two parallel lines:

Once you were not a people, but now you are God's people; once you had not received mercy, but now you have received mercy. (1 Pet. 2:10)

Usually, when Christians tell their testimonies, they focus on that second line. "I was living a life of sin," we say, "but then God showed me mercy." What a glorious story that is.

INTRODUCTION

But it's not the whole story, Peter says. Something else happens in that exact same moment: When we receive mercy, we are also joined to a people. Conversion is corporate. It adds you to a family through adoption.

Maybe we could tell our testimonies like this: "I was living a life of sin, and I wanted nothing to do with other Christians. But then God saved me. He showed me mercy and added me to his family."

Paul tells the same story in Ephesians 2. The first half focuses on our vertical reconciliation with God by grace: "But God . . . raised us up with him and seated us with him in the heavenly places" (2:4, 6). Yet that vertical reconciliation brings with it a horizontal reconciliation too. This is Paul's focus in the second half of Ephesians 2: "But now in Christ Jesus you who once were far off have been brought near by the blood of Christ" (2:13). Notice that this horizontal reconciliation occurred in the same place and at the same time as the vertical reconciliation: when Christ shed his blood on the cross.

Again, conversion is corporate, and the gospel makes us a people. Christ accomplished this—past tense.

This means the Christian life is the church-member life. It means that if missions is all about the gospel, then it's also all about the church. If the gospel and the church are bound up together, then so are missions and the church. This is why all

INTRODUCTION

the authors writing in this church-centered missions project agree that *Christianity is church shaped*.

## Downplaying the Church

Sadly, the Christian life in the West has become more individualistic over the last sixty or seventy years. How? Churches have adopted the devices of the marketplace to attract customers, and a "customer" is hardly the same thing as a "family member." Several generations of missionaries have grown up in these kinds of churches. Seminaries, too, teach pastors and missionaries to adopt pragmatic, marketplace methods. And what we manufacture at home, we export overseas.

As a result, modern missions often overlooks the church. First, missionaries overlook the church for their own lives and discipleship. Many have a sending agency but not a sending church. Once missionaries have been sent, agencies sometimes ignore their church experiences on the field. In extreme cases, agencies sometimes prohibit missionaries from joining a church on the field. People can do something as dramatic as cross an ocean, obtain a residence visa, begin to acquire the local language . . . and yet forsake the churches that already meet in their new home. Such neglect sadly hinders the missionaries' own growth and endurance in the faith. It also hurts their parenting and their marriages.

Second, missionaries overlook the importance of a church for the people they are trying to reach. They see the church, at best, as incidental to their gospel ministry. Some even see it as a hindrance. We think of someone like Ahmed (not his real name), a Muslim from the Arabian Peninsula. Western missionaries shared the gospel with him. He professed faith in Christ. The missionaries engaged him in friendship, encouragement, and discipleship. But they never directed him to a local church. They left Ahmed without pastoral oversight, weekly worship, and church fellowship—no sermons, no ordinances, no means to serve. Instead, they told him that he was a member of an underreached people group, that he faced difficulties others did not, and that it was inevitable and acceptable for him to live as a churchless Christian. Those missionaries have since left the country, and Ahmed has been left to fend for himself spiritually.

Why was Ahmed not folded into the life of a local congregation—whether an Arabic or English congregation, an established or underground one? Partly because the missionaries who shared the gospel with him downplayed the church. They had weak *ecclesiology*, a word which refers to our doctrine and practice of the church. The trouble is, weak ecclesiology leads to weak *missiology*, a word which refers to our doctrine and practice of missions. After all, our missiology

## INTRODUCTION

is downstream from our ecclesiology. The larger lesson here is simple: What we believe about the church will influence how we carry out the Great Commission.

Many missionaries faithfully evangelize and help God's people through difficult contexts, for which we're grateful. But too often the role they give to the church in making disciples is swallowed by pragmatism, minimalism, and neglect. Some missionaries attend churches but remain on the margins. They refuse to join and instead associate only with other missionaries. Some desire to partner with churches overseas but face the disapproval of the mission agencies who sent them. We have both seen this firsthand. Friends have witnessed the same. One pastor friend in Central Asia described to us how the missionaries in his English-language church "seem almost tortured when attending our church." He explained, "They feel like every moment they give to our church community is a moment they are neglecting the people to whom they were sent. It's as if they think faithful church membership and faithful gospel work among other peoples are at odds."

How does this happen? A few ideas:

- Churches at home fail to equip future missionaries with a biblical ecclesiology before sending them to the field.

## INTRODUCTION

- Those same churches then outsource too much of the training responsibilities that can be performed in-house to missions agencies and other parachurch organizations.
- As a result, missionaries arrive on the field and get to work "making disciples," but they do so without regard to biblical conversion or the biblical priorities of preaching and teaching, elder oversight, biblical ordinances, and church membership.

### Downplaying Theology and the Bible

Underlying the minimal ecclesiology in missions is a tendency toward minimal theology in general. This trend is nothing new. In 1970 Walter Chantry lamented that missionaries too often go looking for "the lowest common denominator to which all born-again Christians hold." When they do, the "rest of the Bible will be labelled 'unessential' for missions."[10] A generation later, two other missiologists sound the same warning: "Bad theology leads to bad missions, and bad missions spreads more bad theology."[11] This trend is perpetuated

10  Walter Chantry, *Today's Gospel: Authentic or Synthetic?* (Edinburgh, UK: Banner of Truth, 1970), 3.
11  Chad Vegas and Alex Kocman, *Missions By the Book: How Theology and Missions Walk Together* (Cape Coral, FL: Founders Press, 2021), 2. They continued,

by the popular mantra that "missions is the mother of theology." This book argues the opposite—missions is the *application* of our theology.

Recognizing these trends toward theological minimalism, a group of theologians and missions strategists known as the Southgate Fellowship wrote a document called "Affirmations and Denials Concerning World Mission." It pushes back on the critiques against "traditional" or historic missions that have characterized missions conversations for the past fifty years. The document argues that "many in the study and practice of world mission have strayed methodologically from the sure foundation of Scripture."[12] Some of those

---

"Many of the most adventurous, risk-taking mission workers are trained to check their theology at the door of the sending organization and learn a host of man-centered ministry tactics that stem from cultural relativism. These missionaries are told that the same gospel-centered, doctrine-rich teaching that builds faithful churches in the West won't work elsewhere in the world and that some new and different insight from sociology is needed in non-Western cultures."

12 The Southgate Fellowship, "Affirmations and Denials Concerning World Mission," *Themelios* 45, no. 1 (April 2020): 108. This call to faithful mission, accessible at https://thesouthgatefellowship.org/, was written to "rearticulate biblical mission thought and practice, attempt to locate and expose weaknesses and errors in various contemporary paradigms, and seek to call missiologists, missionaries, mission agencies, and Christ's global church to biblical fidelity in belief, thought, methods, and goals—all in obedience to Jesus Christ, the Lord of the nations."

critiques were on target, as when addressing colonialist mindsets or failures to contextualize. The trouble was that "when the critics threw out pews and hymns and church buildings," one veteran missionary shared in personal conversation with us, "they got rid of everything. The pendulum swung too far."

When good doctrine and the Scriptures are neglected, other forces fill the void. For instance, *movement-driven missions* is an approach to missions that aims at starting movements, as the name implies. It depends on techniques designed to spark revivals in underreached contexts. Its goal is easy reproducibility and rapid multiplication, usually involving superficial and cursory biblical instruction. Movement-driven missions tends to focus on techniques and methods that produce visible results with the hope that these visible manifestations are accompanied by spiritual life. As a result, though visible movements might begin, too often they appear to be works of the flesh rather than the Spirit. They rely on the powers of psychology and everyday human group dynamics, just like any other trend that comes and goes in a culture. Advocates of Church Planting Movements, which is one brand of movement-driven missions, promote them as "the most effective means in the world" to bring lost millions to Christ. They emphasize speed, explosive numbers, and immediately

## INTRODUCTION

measurable success.[13] They also criticize careful attention to ecclesiology and the ordinary means of grace as the "slow to grow approach."[14]

A church-centered missions paradigm, on the other hand, encourages conversions and builds churches though "teaching everything Jesus commanded" (Matt. 28:20). That's why another one of the planks mentioned in the preface of this book is that *missions is Bible led*. It's Bible led in that the Bible tells us how to do missions, and it's Bible led in that it treats the Bible itself as essential for making disciples.

On that score, Christians have long referred to the "ordinary means of grace." Churches should not work to make disciples through extraordinary means, through dynamic and exciting new techniques never mentioned in the Bible. Rather, they should use the ordinary, everyday practices like preaching, teaching, singing, praying, and practicing the ordinances. None of this requires fancy marketing methods,

---

13 David Garrison, *Church Planting Movements: How God Is Redeeming a Lost World* (Midlothian, VA: WIGtake Resources, 2004), 28.

14 For example, we are told by movement proponents that "traditional methods take too long, cost too much, and bring about minimal cultural transformation." Aila Tasse and L. Michael Corley, "The Way of Life: Transference of Spiritual DNA within Movements in East Africa," in *Motus Dei: The Movement of God to Disciple the Nations*, ed. Warrick Farah (Littleton, CO: William Carey, 2021), 236.

## INTRODUCTION

a PhD in cultural anthropology, or a "how-to" study guide. Everything missionaries absolutely need is in the Bible.

## Church-Centered Missions

Both of us are pastors of international, English-speaking churches in Muslim countries. John spent two years pastoring in Washington, DC. For the last twenty years, he has pastored the Evangelical Christian Church of Dubai in the United Arab Emirates (UAE). Scott pastors the Union Church of Istanbul, Turkey. Prior to that, he spent a decade serving as a pioneer church planter in Central Asia, after which he helped to run the International Mission Board's training program and earned a PhD in missiology. He also served as Director of Global Outreach at McLean Bible Church in Virginia.

We've seen firsthand the crucial role of healthy churches in fulfilling the Great Commission—as overseas pastors, sending-church pastors, and missionaries. Throughout this book, we'll share some of our experiences. We'll tell a number of stories from our lives, friendships, and work on the mission field. Most names and some details have been changed to protect individuals' privacy. We begin *Prioritizing the Church in Missions* by considering what the church *is*—a subject about which there is growing confusion. Without clear thinking on the church, missions becomes a game of blindman's bluff.

In other words, if we don't know what a church is, we won't know if we've succeeded or not in our mission. Missionaries must have a clear vision of what to replicate on the field, and the Bible is our authoritative, sufficient guide. It gives clear guidance for the church in every context.

In chapter 2, we'll define *missions*. In accord with the series as a whole, we define missions as churches sending qualified workers across linguistic, geographic, or cultural barriers to start or strengthen churches, especially in places where Christ has not been named. There are many other good things Christians can do overseas (disaster relief, orphan care, fighting HIV), but if we do those things in the same way as UNICEF or the Red Crescent, our work does not qualify as missions.

Chapters 3, 4, and 5 will unpack the core of our argument, that churches are:

- The *origin* of missions activity. Local congregations should train and equip future missionaries, and they—not parachurch organizations or mystical guidance from the Holy Spirit—should give primary oversight to the mission.
- The *means* of missions activity. "Making disciples" is the job of all churches everywhere. Missionaries

overseas aren't "free agents," but should join a local church. Likewise, the people they reach with the gospel should become members of a church, where they will learn by teaching and example to obey all that Jesus commanded.

- The *end* of missions. By referring to the end of missions, we don't mean to discount the *ultimate* end of missions—the praise and glory of God. We are referring to the earthly end for which a missionary works: starting and strengthening a church. Individual conversions are not enough. Those converts need to be joined to a church because the Christian life is the church life. We affirm with the Southgate Fellowship that "the goal of missions is inextricably tied to the visible church—the means and end of Christ's work, through which God's Spirit by his Word gathers and perfects his people."[15]

Finally, in chapter 6 we will argue that missions works best when churches cooperate to see the gospel flourish in spiritually starved places. This is another plank in the church-centered missions paradigm: *Missions works best when churches*

15  Southgate Fellowship, "Affirmations and Denials," 125.

*work together*. In the New Testament and throughout history, the gospel sped forward when the churches greeted one another (Rom. 16:16), prayed for one another (Eph. 6:18), supported one another financially (2 Cor. 8:19), and cooperated in sending missionaries (3 John 6–8). Such cooperation glorifies God and empowers cross-cultural gospel work.

Before departing for India in 1793, William Carey preached his farewell sermon at Harvey Lane Baptist Church amid tearful good-byes. In those days, many missionaries packed all their possessions in their coffins. They had no plan to return. One historian recorded, "In June of 1793, from the deck of the Kron Princessa Maria, Carey saw England for the last time, at the commencement of his 15,000 mile journey to India."[16]

Six months earlier, Carey and eleven other pastors had formed the Baptist Missionary Society. The society was comprised of a handful of congregations in the English Midlands who were "poor and unknown to the wider world."[17] Their pledges amounted to a few dollars. The obstacles were immense. When Carey landed overseas, he plunged into an abyss of hostility. He had none of the training and support we have come to rely on in modern missions. Instead, Carey

16 Iain Murray, *The Puritan Hope* (Edinburgh: Banner of Truth, 1971), 138.

17 Murray, *Puritan Hope*, 138.

INTRODUCTION

consciously depended on those banded-together congregations' ongoing support and prayer.

At his send-off, a speaker called the occasion a "hoped for, dreaded day." Some felt as if Carey were descending into a deep pit. One of the society leaders, Andrew Fuller, recalled, "Before he went down . . . he, as it seemed to me, took an oath from each of us, at the mouth of the pit, to this effect—that 'while we lived, we should never let go of the rope.'"[18]

In faith, the society drafted a letter of greeting to Carey's future Hindu inquirers: "From Asia sounded out the word of the Lord into Europe. Glad shall we be to have that joyful sound reverberate to Asia again, and to extend to every other part of the earth!"[19] During the ensuing forty years, that's exactly what happened—the gospel reverberated back into Asia "again." Why "again"? Because the gospel had originally come from Asia to Europe, when the church at Antioch sent Paul on his second journey (Acts 15:35; 16:11). Centuries later, the cooperating churches of the English Midlands sent the gospel back through William Carey. In both cases, local churches worked hand in hand.

18 Andrew Fuller, *The Complete Works of Rev. Andrew Fuller: With a Memoir of His Life*, ed. Joseph Belcher, 3rd ed. (Philadelphia, 1845), 1:68.
19 George, *Faithful Witness*, 77.

## INTRODUCTION

Today, flying from the United States to where Carey and Zwemer pioneered takes only fourteen hours. We put our belongings in our suitcases, not our coffins. In global cities throughout the world, people now come and go with regularity. Christians already live in cities like Bangkok, Delhi, and Istanbul. They live among the local people, gather in churches, and worship Christ in many languages. Globalization has changed the missions landscape. But even so, the church remains the origin, the means, and the end of missions.

# 1

# What Is the Church?

A few years ago, I (John) visited Jerusalem with my Palestinian friend Danny. We stood on the Mount of Olives and looked down at the site of the Jerusalem temple. Where the temple once stood, there is now a Muslim shrine called the Dome of the Rock.

You can walk the whole area in fifteen minutes. Down the Mount, through the cemetery, past the ancient olive groves where many believe Jesus prayed the night he was betrayed. We walked up the hill into the Old City, then to the entrance of the mosque. From a historical standpoint it was fascinating. As a reader of the Bible, I gained perspective to piece things together. But I didn't feel any nearer to the Lord. It's not as if God gives you extra points for walking where Jesus walked.

# CHAPTER I

Of course, many traditions disagree. There's a mystical appeal to the history, the architecture, the incense, and the inaccessible rooms. I saw people lying prostrate on the marble slab where Jesus was supposedly buried, kissing the worn-away stones. I traveled through tunnels approaching the Western Wall, where the security tightened up. I remembered the photographs of world leaders tucking prayer notes in the wall's crevices. I emptied my pockets at the metal detectors and walked into one of the most sacred religious sites in the world. A sign greeted us: "Dear Visitors: You are approaching the holy site of the Western Wall where the Divine Presence always rests."

For many, this is ground zero for meeting with God. It doesn't get any holier than this. But is that really true? Didn't the destruction of the temple in AD 70 prove that the divine presence had *left*? If the Western Wall is no longer the epicenter of the divine presence on earth, then what is?

The writer of Hebrews tells believers, "You have come to Mount Zion and to the city of the living God, the heavenly Jerusalem, and to innumerable angels in festal gathering, and to the assembly [*ekklesia*] of the firstborn who are enrolled in heaven" (Heb. 12:22–23).

Ground zero is no longer at the Jerusalem temple. It's now the church of Jesus Christ, a heavenly gathering ("the *assembly* of the firstborn who are enrolled in heaven") made visible through local churches. Just as God assembled Israel at Mount Sinai both to receive the Law and to celebrate the sacred feasts, so he assembles his people today. Hebrews describes an end-times gathering that is mirrored on earth every Lord's Day. Every Sunday, we participate in heavenly worship that has already begun. Our churches may seem ordinary, marked by warts and blemishes, but they are the place where the divine presence rests on earth.

This is why the church matters for missions. God's glory goes public through local churches as they display "the manifold wisdom of God" (Eph. 3:10). Preaching makes the gospel *audible*; biblical churches make the gospel *visible*. They show what it looks like when gospel truth transforms people. When Jesus commanded his people to "make disciples of all nations, baptizing them" (Matt. 28:19), he meant into visible, local expressions of the end-times, heavenly assembly.

What is a church? We agree with this definition from the companion volume *Prioritizing Missions in the Church*: A church is a congregation of baptized Christians who have covenanted to gather weekly for preaching the Bible, celebrating the ordinances, loving the saints, witnessing to the lost, and, in all this, glorifying God.[1]

---

1 Aaron Menikoff and Harshit Singh, *Prioritizing Missions in the Church* (Wheaton, IL: Crossway, 2025), 7.

CHAPTER 1

## Judges 22 Churches

Samuel Zwemer was described as "the blazing herald of the gospel."[2] In the late 1800s, he traveled the Arabian coastline, distributed Bibles, conversed in public markets, endured suspicion and scorn, provided amateur medical care, and even extracted teeth. Zwemer said, "In a place where dentistry is practiced by the use of wedges, hammers and tongs and where they fill a hollow tooth with melted lead to ease pain, I have won a score of friends by less painful methods."[3] It was a hard and often thankless calling. The local people were suspicious and, when they heard his message, openly hostile. Zwemer recalled times when "colporteurs [booksellers] were arrested; the Bible shop sealed up; books confiscated; and a guard placed at the door of the house occupied by the missionaries."[4] Through it all, Zwemer never budged from

2   J. Christy Wilson, *Apostle to Islam: A Biography of Samuel M. Zwemer* (Grand Rapids, MI: Baker, 1952), 13.

3   Wilson, *Apostle to Islam*, 47. A few decades later, Dorothy Van Ess described a similar experience of her husband, John, when he was conducting a clinic on the Pirate Coast (modern-day UAE), extracting the tooth of a "burly" Arab woman. "He said he almost had to put his knee on her chest to get it out, and was sure he must have broken her jaw, but she wiped her face with her veil, pointed to the other side of her mouth, and said, 'Here's another!'" quoted in Lewis R. Scudder III, *The Arabian Mission's Story: In Search of Abraham's Other Son* (Grand Rapids, MI: Eerdmans, 1995), 164.

4   Wilson, *Apostle to Islam*, 45.

his main aim "to plant the Cross wherever the Crescent holds sway."[5]

After years of ministry in Arabia, Zwemer explained why he thought Muslims were so hard to reach. This was his first reason: "From the very beginning the examples of Christ's way of life that they had before them were so repellent as to widen the breach rather than to bridge it. . . . Christ's way of life in Muslim lands has never won multitudes because it has never been lived among them on a noble scale over a considerable period of time."[6]

In other words, bad churches made evangelism harder. In Zwemer's experience, instead of shining cities on a hill, too many churches were weak and worldly, projecting a confusing, even "repellent" vision for the Christian life.

To this day, unhealthy churches are powerful antimissionary forces. They confuse the world about the gospel, and they hinder cross-cultural evangelism.[7]

---

5   Wilson, *Apostle to Islam*, 13.

6   Samuel Zwemer, *Islam and the Cross: Selections from "The Apostle to Islam"* (Phillipsburg, PA: P&R Publishing, 2002) 56.

7   Movement-driven missions agrees that bad churches are a problem. "The reality is that Christianity does not have a good name in most of the world." David Watson and Paul Watson, *Contagious Disciple-Making* (Nashville: Thomas Nelson, 2014), 25. We agree with the Watsons' diagnosis but not on their solution.

## CHAPTER I

Today's movement-driven missions is, in part, a reaction against *un*healthy churches and missions practices. For too long, Western churches have had an "export problem"—sending missionaries who put up unnecessary roadblocks to the gospel. For these missionaries, when they think of "the church," they think of buildings and steeples and pews. Put simply, they fail to contextualize. We agree with some of these critiques, and we recognize the baggage Christianity carries. Even the word *church*, as Jonathan Leeman explained, "has spent centuries, like a slow meandering river, picking up all kinds of flotsam and sediment, from the idea of a building to the idea of a hierarchical structure (e.g., Roman Catholic *Church*, Evangelical Lutheran *Church*)."[8] Still, while acknowledging the baggage, we prefer *church* over the weaker term *fellowship* or, worse, *movement* or *cell*. The latter two terms have subversive political connotations in some parts of the world.

Thankfully, missionaries have learned important lessons from our forebears' ministry mistakes. We don't know any missionaries today who are agents of colonial influence or who insist on church buildings with dedicated baptisteries.

8    Jonathan Leeman, *One Assembly: Rethinking the Multi-Site and Multi-Service Church Models* (Wheaton, IL: Crossway, 2020), 20; cf. Janet Eastham, "Church of England dropping word 'church' to be more 'modern,'" *The Telegraph*, Aug. 16, 2024. https://www.telegraph.co.uk/.

But in much of contemporary missions, the pendulum has swung too far in the other direction. Too much of modern missions now downplays the church, redefines it, or ignores it altogether.

Consider these quotes from movement-driven literature:

- "I can't give you a good definition of the church, but when I see one, I know it."[9]
- "The Scriptures don't give a precise definition, so I'm not going to do what God has not done."[10]
- "There is no single biblical model of what a church must be."[11]
- "The NT provides a flexible ecclesiology and provides no neat definition of the form of church."[12]

In these authors' minds, ecclesiology is shrink-wrapped down to this: "To confess with one's mouth and believe in

9  Watson and Watson, *Contagious Disciple-Making*, 160.
10  Neil Cole, "Organic Church," in *Perspectives on the World Christian Movement*, 4th ed., ed. Ralph Winter and Stephen Hawthorne (Pasadena, CA: William Carey Library, 2009), 644.
11  Steve Smith with Ying Kai, *T4T: A Discipleship Re-Revolution* (Monument, CO: WIGTAKE Resources, 2011), 250.
12  Warrick Farah, "Movements Today: A Primer from Multiple Perspectives" in *Motus Dei: The Movement of God to Disciple the Nations*, ed. Warrick Farah (Littleton, CO: William Carey, 2021), 10.

## CHAPTER I

one's heart that Jesus is Lord—that is all there is. Nothing else really matters. All else is to be held lightly. Everything else is negotiable."[13]

Pragmatism guides movement-driven missions. Too many of its practitioners seem to say that if we can just figure out a strategy that works, then we can "reverse engineer" it and reproduce spiritual results.[14] As David and Paul Watson wrote, "Stick with the process and there will be fruit."[15]

But pragmatism and man-centered ecclesiology result in false conversions, weak sheep, and a distortion of Jesus's name among the nations. The results are disastrous. As Mack Stiles writes, "What we have in so many places around the globe is not 'Acts 29' churches but what I call 'Judges 22' churches: churches that do what is right in their own eyes (Judg. 21:25)."[16] Unhealthy churches on the field are antimissions.

---

13 Charles Van Engen, *Mission on the Way: Issues in Mission Theology* (Grand Rapids: Baker Academic, 1996), 184, quoted in David Garner, "High Stakes: Insider Movement Hermeneutics and the Gospel," *Themelios* 37, no. 2 (2012): 262.

14 David Garrison, *Church Planting Movements: How God Is Redeeming a Lost World* (Midlothian, VA: WIGtake Resources, 2004), 11.

15 Watson and Watson, *Contagious Disciple-Making*, 114.

16 Mack Stiles, *Evangelism: How the Whole Church Speaks of Jesus* (Wheaton, IL: Crossway, 2014), 69.

## Special Agents

In 2017, ten American evangelists from a student missions organization moved to the most Islamic city in the UAE to evangelize university students. These student-evangelists were told to conceal their identity and mission from the churches that met in the city. Luke, one of the ten, recalled, "We were special agents who were going to get the Great Commission done. No one could get in our way."

The team thought of themselves as a family. They had a "team covenant" that outlined expectations and even a disciplinary process. "We were functioning as a church," Luke said. There were no biblically qualified elders or church ordinances.

When students professed faith, they weren't directed to a local church and baptized. Instead, they were assured of their salvation "on the spot." Team leaders would bake a birthday cake, celebrating the student's new birth. Luke recalled, "It was candles, singing, the whole nine yards. The strange thing was that the person wasn't even there!" Due to security concerns, these new believers couldn't attend the team meeting.

Over the course of the first year, ten people professed faith. But Luke recalled, "By the end of the year we had contact with none of them. . . . Our focus was starting a 'movement' on the campus. That was the lingo. Students sharing with

## CHAPTER I

students in a rapid-fire way. . . . We had met a huge swath of people, but with no way of following up. It was exhausting, spiritually unhealthy."

In time, Luke decided to join a local church. This "began to create some issues" with team leadership. "I felt like I was in disobedience."

But over time Luke grew spiritually, and evangelistic opportunities multiplied through the church. Luke learned that the local church doesn't compete with missions efforts.

In fact, the Great Commission (Matt. 28:18–20) can't be fulfilled apart from the Great Constitution (16:17–19). The same Lord who commanded "go and make disciples" also assured, against all opposition, that "I will build my church." The church is central to God's global purposes.

Thankfully, the Scriptures offer several lessons about what a church is. We want to highlight three.

### What the Church Is

#### *A Gathering*

First, the church in the New Testament is a gathering. It's not a building or an event but an assembly of God's people. Sometimes the assembly is depicted as universal (e.g., Matt. 16:18) or heavenly (e.g., Heb. 12:23), but in the vast majority of instances, the word *church* refers to a local assembly (e.g., Rom. 16:5).

The New Testament warns against "neglecting to meet together, as is the habit of some" (Heb. 10:25). But in some missions circles today, gathering with the church is discouraged. One missiologist asks,

> Must Buddhists, Hindus, and Muslims become Christians in order to belong to Christ? Do they have to be incorporated into church organizations that are utterly alien to their religious traditions? Do they have to call themselves Christians? Do they have to adopt Christian customs and rites which are necessarily Western?[17]

The implied answer to these rhetorical questions is no.

The church is not "necessarily Western." It began in the Near East, and its origin reaches back to the ancient *qahal* (Deut. 4:10), the assembly of Israel. In the Old Testament, gatherings of God's people were the fundamental expression of worship. As Christopher Ash writes, "Israel is not a

---

17 Brad Gill, "03/22/15—AM service—Missions Conference Speaker," First Baptist Church of St. John's, March 22, 2015, quoted in Chad Vegas and Alex Kocman, *Missions By the Book: How Theology and Missions Walk Together* (Cape Coral, FL: Founders Press, 2021), 58.

collection of individuals who sometimes assemble; it is an assembly whose members may sometimes be dispersed."[18] The assembly of Israel established the pattern of the new covenant assembly. People need not come into *Western* Christianity to belong to Christ, but they must come into *biblical* Christianity.

The Insider Movement (IM) is a method in modern missions that undermines the church. It teaches Muslims who come to faith in Christ that they can remain anonymously *inside* the religious structures of Islam—still attending mosque, reciting Muslim prayers and creeds, revering Mohammad—while secretly following Christ. As David Garner critiques IM, "Muslims stay Muslim, Buddhists stay Buddhist, Hindus stay Hindu."[19] Leaving one's religious identity isn't necessary. One supporter of IM explains, "Christ calls people to change their hearts, not their religions."[20] Therefore, according to this view, the church is not essential; it's better for believers to remain in the mosque.

---

18 Christopher Ash, *The Priority of Preaching* (Fearn, UK: Christian Focus, 2009), 80.

19 David Garner, "High Stakes: Insider Movement Hermeneutics and the Gospel," *Themelios* 37, no. 2 (2012): 265.

20 Stan Guthrie, *Missions in the Third Millenium: 21 Key Trends for the 21st Century*, rev. ed. (Eugene, OR: Wipf and Stock, 2014), quoted in David Garner, "High Stakes," 254.

But Jesus assumed that his followers would be *publicly* aligned with him. As he warned his disciples, "They will put you out of the synagogues" (John 16:2). Remaining secret wasn't an option. "Whoever is ashamed of me and of my words in this adulterous and sinful generation, of him will the Son of Man also be ashamed when he comes in the glory of his Father with the holy angels" (Mark 8:38). Mixing hidden devotion to Christ with false religion raises a question: "What fellowship has light with darkness?" (2 Cor. 6:14). We agree with Doug Coleman, who says, "Attending Friday prayers and prostrating toward Mecca is forbidden for the believer in Jesus, even if that prayer is inwardly directed toward the Lord."[21] Why? Because the person participating in such activities is publicly professing adherence to a false god, even if the heart is not.

Samuel Zwemer criticized "faith in the heart, but lips that are silent."[22] This doesn't mean that converts must necessarily endanger themselves by attending conspicuously public gatherings. Nor does it require them to jeopardize their continued presence in the community. In some contexts, an

---

21 Elliot Clark, *Mission Affirmed: Recovering the Missionary Motivation of Paul* (Wheaton, IL: Crossway, 2022), 177.

22 Samuel Zwemer, "A Word to Secret Believers," in *Chrislam: How Missionaries Are Promoting an Islamized Gospel*, rev. ed., ed. Joshua Lingel (Garden Grove, CA: i2 Ministries, 2012), 307. Zwemer also wrote, "The Arab proverb says that the hand cannot hold two watermelons. The heart cannot hold two religions."

## CHAPTER I

"underground" church may be necessary. Certainly Christians in such situations need wisdom. But believers are "sojourners and exiles" in this world. We should expect to be "rejected by men" (1 Pet. 2:4, 11).

In some parts of the world, identifying with the church may result in backlash. But that was the case in the New Testament. Former Jews suffered because they left their family religion and embraced Jesus as Lord. They faced reproach, loss of property, even imprisonment (Heb. 10:33–34). But what does the author of Hebrews say? "Don't neglect meeting together." And later: "Therefore let us go to him outside the camp and bear the reproach he endured" (10:25; 13:13).

When believers go to Christ "outside the camp," they join his assembled people. Throughout history, and sometimes at great cost, the church has always gathered.

### A People

Yet the church is not just a gathering, like we find in any random crowd. It's a gathering of God's people who have been marked off and publicly affirmed by the ordinances. Peter tells us, "You are a chosen race, a royal priesthood, a holy nation, a people for his own possession" (1 Pet. 2:9).

Peter applies these Old Testament titles to the scattered churches of Asia Minor because God's true people have been reconstituted through the death and resurrection of Jesus Christ. Now Gentiles, once strangers to God's promises, are welcome: "Once you were not a people, but now you are God's people" (1 Pet. 2:10). The global church is the fulfillment of God's promises to Israel.

From the beginning, God's purpose has been to glorify himself not through isolated individuals but through a community of believers. In the garden of Eden, God established the first family. In his covenant with Abraham, God promised to make him into a great nation. In the Sinai covenant, God pledged himself to the whole Israelite community: "I will walk among you and will be your God, and you shall be my people" (Lev. 26:12).

Israel would prove unfaithful, so God would reject them. And yet, he would eventually come in the person of his Son to reassemble the true people of God: I will build my assembly—my church (Matt. 16:18).

Reem, an Emirati university student, visited my (John's) church in Dubai a few times. She was on a self-guided field trip for a class on "Religion and Society." As part of her course, she visited different religious centers and drew comparisons with Islam. What differences did Reem note between her mosque and our church? The architecture was different, and the singing got her attention. But her main observation concerned the

CHAPTER I

people. She reported: "Everyone seemed to be friends with everyone. . . . This church is more than just a community or a congregation of people; it is more like a family."

God has saved us not into an event or a tradition, but into a family. Edmund Clowney said, "Jesus' true family was not bound by the blood of physical descent, but by his own blood, given on the cross."[23] The gospel creates a culture like no other. Church planters should live on the field not as lone rangers but in biblical community. And those who come to faith through their ministries should not remain isolated but be incorporated into the church, the people of God.

### A Temple

When the temple was dedicated in Jerusalem, the glory of the Lord descended. But even then, Solomon acknowledged in his prayer of dedication, "Heaven and the highest heaven, cannot contain [the LORD]; how much less this house [temple] that I have built!" (1 Kings 8:27).

Centuries later Jesus would say at that very spot, "Destroy this temple, and in three days I will raise it up" (John 2:19). Jesus became the new dwelling place in whom "the whole fullness of deity dwells bodily" (Col. 2:9). Amazingly, Paul

23 Edmund Clowney, *How Jesus Transforms the Ten Commandments* (Phillipsburg, NJ: P&R, 2007), 68.

later applies that same temple imagery to those who belong to Christ: "In him you also are being built together into a dwelling place for God by the Spirit" (Eph. 2:22).

This dwelling is not a shrine (like the Dome of the Rock) or a hallowed ruin (like the Western Wall). God's new dwelling place is his assembled people. Christ dwells in our midst, in the church, by his Spirit. Now, through Christ, not only are all the peoples of the earth *admitted* to the temple, but they are "living stones," the very building blocks that form it (1 Pet. 2:5).

This spiritual dynamic impressed Mehdi and Shabnam, an Iranian couple who walked into my church building in Dubai, looking for information about Jesus. They had been investigating different religions: Zoroastrianism, Buddhism, Kabbalah. Each they found wanting. Shabnam recalled, "I never had the feeling that I could talk to God, because I didn't follow all the rules." Someone explained the good news of Jesus Christ to them and introduced them to members of our church. They began attending, hearing God's word, and getting to know people from dozens of different nationalities. In time, they believed the gospel and were baptized. As they recalled, "It was unbelievable. God touched our hearts!"

Since Christ is among his people, the church is Jesus's cross-cultural evangelism plan. Mehdi and Shabnam not only

## CHAPTER I

*heard* the gospel, but they *saw* Christ in the members' love for one another. Whether CEOs or construction laborers, God's people reached out to them in gospel friendship. The church is not a ritualistic show; it is a spiritual temple in which there are no expats, no foreigners, no aliens. "You are fellow citizens with the saints and members of the household of God" (Eph. 2:19). The church is the confirming echo of the gospel.[24]

Sadly, movement-driven missions muffles that echo by encouraging converts to stay within their subgroups or castes. Such approaches are considered more likely to result in "People Movements" because people naturally "prefer to join churches whose members look, talk, and act like themselves."[25] One pioneer of these tactics, Donald McGavran, urges, "Establish churches made up largely of taxi drivers. . . . The congregation has a natural, built-in social cohesion. Everybody feels at home."[26] They might feel at home, but that just reinforces

24 For a helpful description of a "culture of evangelism" in the life of a church, see Stiles's *Evangelism*. Intentional *corporate* evangelism is one reason Jesus prayed for unity among God's people: "So that the world may believe that you have sent me" (John 17:21).

25 Donald McGavran, *Understanding Church Growth*, 3rd ed., rev. and ed. Wagner (Grand Rapids, MI: Eerdmans, 1990), 227.

26 Donald McGavran, "A Church in Every People: Plain Talk About a Difficult Subject," in *Perspectives on the World Christian Movement*, 4th ed., ed. Ralph Winter and Stephen Hawthorne (Pasadena, CA: William Carey Library, 2009), 629. Compare Zambian pastor Conrad Mbewe's counsel: "We must never limit

society's status quo. Assembling a crowd with shared interests doesn't require the Holy Spirit.

But in the new spiritual temple, Christ has "broken down the dividing wall of hostility" between Jew and Gentile, creating "one new man" (Eph. 2:14–15). This united spiritual body cuts across racial, cultural, and socioeconomic lines, and it's made visible through local churches.

## What the Church Does

Missionaries must know how to define a church. You cannot reproduce what you cannot define. We believe the Bible guides the church in every context. Thankfully, God has spoken not only about what the church *is*, but what the church *does*.[27]

### *Preaching and Teaching*

What does a church do? For starters, it centers on preaching and teaching.

---

our church's membership to one tribe or one ethnic group." *God's Design for the Church: A Guide for African Pastors and Ministry Leaders* (Wheaton, IL: Crossway, 2020), 31.

27 John Hammett lists a variety of church activities, including prayer, fellowship, serving widows and the needy, and spreading the gospel, showing that churches are "dynamic, purposeful assemblies." Hammet, *Biblical Foundations for Baptist Churches* (Grand Rapids, MI: Kregel, 2005), 29. Here we will focus on five other activities of the church.

## CHAPTER I

Over breakfast a missionary explained his team's new approach to reaching Muslims in a closed North African country. He rejoiced that they had been able to start more than a dozen Discovery Bible Studies among the locals. But there were no Christians in these groups. He and the other missionaries intentionally stayed away. They agreed with the Watsons: "When working with lost people, we have to avoid falling into the role of explaining Scripture. If we do, we become the authority rather than allowing Scripture to be the authority."[28]

But this is precisely why churches should give themselves to preaching that's dedicated to exposing God's word. The preacher wields legitimate authority only because he is "rightly handling the word of truth" (2 Tim. 2:15). Consider the early church practice:

- "And they devoted themselves to the apostles' teaching" (Acts 2:42).

---

28 Watson and Watson, *Contagious Disciple-Making*, 149. This is still a widely held view. Missions writer and movements advocate David Coles, for example, explains that "CPM proponents . . . eschew the common approach of 'authoritatively explaining the meaning of a text.'" Coles, "Addressing Theological and Missiological Objections to CPM/DMM" in *Motus Dei: The Movement of God to Disciple the Nations*, ed. Warrick Farah (Littleton, CO: William Carey, 2021) 43. Evangelistic Bible studies are valuable tools, but they require someone who is able to teach, answer questions, and defend the gospel.

- "He stayed a year and six months, teaching the word of God among them" (Acts 18:11).
- "Command and teach these things" (1 Tim. 4:11).
- "As for you, teach what accords with sound doctrine" (Titus 2:1).

Despite this biblical emphasis, one missionary in Honduras concluded that preaching was "ineffective." Instead, he used "dramatic Bible reading, songs with music and lyrics composed by nationals, poems, symbols and storytelling."[29]

Pastors face pressure to provide entertainment or social commentary. But when the Bible is no longer front and center, the members atrophy and the vision blurs.

A missions-centered church, on the other hand, is committed to sound preaching. This is true for a "sending" church from a gospel-rich part of the world and a "receiving" church in a needy part of the world. Preaching propels the missions enterprise.

Faithful preaching will look different in a living room with eight people than in a church meeting hall with three hundred people. But its goal remains the same: to expose the

---

29 George Patterson, "The Spontaneous Multiplication of Churches," in *Perspectives on the World Christian Movement*, 4th ed., ed. Ralph Winter and Stephen Hawthorne (Pasadena, CA: William Carey Library, 2009), 635.

## CHAPTER I

meaning of the passage and then press it home to the hearer. Shepherds feed their sheep through preaching, the food leads to growth, and the growth leads to evangelism.

A small house church gathered in Iraq. A missionary named Karson recalled, "There was regular preaching from the beginning," including series in Ephesians and the Sermon on the Mount. It looked different from what happens in larger churches. The preacher sat in a circle with the others, for example, and the smaller setting allowed for more interaction. "But it wasn't a discussion," Karson said. "It was one preaching to many."

Karson had heard the common critiques of expositional preaching on the mission field. Such preaching, he had been told, requires seminary training. It can't be done. But the fruit of this preaching was clear: Several Muslims came to Christ. One even became a preacher himself!

I've heard critics object that expositional preaching is too *Western*. It won't work in story-telling environments like the Middle East or Central Asia. But exposition began in the East! Five hundred years before Christ, priests and scribes read God's word to men, women, and children. They read "clearly, and they gave the sense, so that the people understood the reading" (Neh. 8:8). This method carried over into the synagogue and eventually the early church. Jesus read Scripture in the Nazareth synagogue and then sat down to preach and explain (Luke 4:21). So did the apostle Paul in the Mediterranean synagogue. He "reasoned" with and persuaded people from the Scriptures (Acts 17:2).

Exposition is not a style—it's the biblical method. It applies in Kurdistan and Kashmir and Korea because it comes from the word of God. Preaching creates the church, and the church drives the Great Commission through preaching.

### Baptism

But churches must do more than preach, otherwise they'll be no different than a Christian conference full of anonymous attendees. Churches must also identify themselves and their members through the ordinances.

I (John) received a message about a Kuwaiti convert who desired to come to Dubai to be baptized. He was a high-profile, public figure, and he feared associating with believers there in Kuwait. Would we baptize him if he flew out and visited us over a weekend?

The answer was no. Not because we didn't care about him or didn't want to encourage his faith. The problem was that he misunderstood baptism. It's not merely one's private expression of allegiance to Christ. It's not a unilateral declaration: "I'm on Team Jesus." Baptism involves two parties:

CHAPTER I

It's a *church's* act and an *individual's* act. The individual confesses; the church affirms that confession. And since this brother didn't live in Dubai, we could hardly commit to him as a church.

Jesus gave the keys of the kingdom to congregations—the only institution with the authority to bind and loose, that is, to affirm a believer's faith and receive him or her into the family (Matt. 18:18). If you read through Matthew's Gospel, you should notice that Matthew links the Great Commission in Matthew 28 back to Matthew 16 and 18, where Jesus gives the apostles and then local churches the authority of the keys to bind and loose. In other words, we need to read the Great Commission in light of the authority Jesus gives churches in Matthew 16 and 18.[30] The Great Commission is a church text because the authority to make disciples and baptize disciples into Jesus's name belongs to churches.

Sure enough, this is what we see in Acts and the Epistles. Churches baptize. Peter preached, "Repent and be baptized"

---

30 Jonathan Leeman writes, "Jesus establishes baptism in Matthew 28. Yet several textual clues tell us to read Matthew 28 in light of Matthew 16 and 18. Presumably, the ones who bind and loose in heaven and earth (Matt. 18) are subject to the one with all authority in heaven and earth (Matt. 28). Presumably, the ones who gather in his name (Matt. 18) are the ones to baptize in his name (Matt. 28). And, presumably, the ones with whom he dwells now (Matt. 18) are the ones with whom he will dwell always (Matt. 28)." Leeman, *One Assembly*, 61–62.

(Acts 2:38). A few verses later, we learn that three thousand are baptized and "added to their number" (2:42). When Paul writes the churches in Rome, he assumes all have been baptized (Rom. 6:2). Their submersion in water symbolized not only cleansing from sin but also union with Christ in his death, burial, and resurrection (6:3–4). It was the sign of entry, the front door into the church.[31]

In the end, we met with the Kuwaiti believer, encouraged him, talked about counting the cost, and pointed him to a biblical church near his home. We understood his potential peril, and we assured him the church in Kuwait would care for him with discretion. We didn't want to encourage him toward a lifetime of isolation from God's people.

In a polytheistic Hindu context, taking an interest in Jesus Christ is not necessarily a problem. After all, there are millions of gods in Hinduism. But the flashpoint, the line in the sand, is baptism. An Indian pastor in a majority Hindu city observed, "Intuitively, they know that baptism means a shift in allegiance." Often, persecution starts not at conversion but after baptism. This is when converts need their new church family to stand with them.

---

31  The Ethiopian eunuch's baptism (Acts 8:38) was the exception that proves the rule. During a transitional phase of redemptive history, he was going to a place where there was no church.

CHAPTER I

Some missionaries today question whether baptism is required. One reports, "Millions are worshipping Jesus in India, but they are not being baptized because they don't want to join the Western fold." In his view, baptism is "cultural suicide," requiring believers to "leave their Hindu world."[32]

Other missionaries go to the other extreme. They don't baptize individual believers upon their profession of faith; they baptize entire groups. Donald McGavran criticized ministry where "all seekers are carefully screened" before admission into the church. Instead of doing church "the slow way," McGavran encouraged "group decisions."[33] Another missionary became impatient with one-by-one baptisms: "At first I acted as though a big buzzard were perched on my shoulder just waiting to pounce on our converts that fell away; I delayed baptism to make sure they were 'safe.' . . . I soon saw, though, that the very reason many fell away was *my* distrust." This missionary shamed himself for not believing that whole groups of people hastily baptized were actually born again. Giving up that "distrust," he embraced sloppy methods and justified himself: "That's the funny thing about God's grace; he wants us to let it slop over on the unworthy."[34] He decided

32 Gill, "03/22/15—AM service—Missions Conference Speaker."

33 McGavran, "A Church in Every People," 627.

34 Patterson, "Spontaneous Multiplication of Churches," 639.

that baptizing entire groups (or families) who show initial interest in "obeying Jesus" (but without a credible profession of faith) is worth the risk that some are not truly regenerate.

This is a recipe for nominal Christianity and syncretism. When missiology downplays the church, gospel witness becomes confused. The fruit is rotten. As one observer of early twentieth-century missions work in Russia recalled, "Heathens before their baptism, they were still heathens after it, and are so till the present day. The fault, in my opinion, lies at the door of our missionaries."[35]

Jesus instructs his followers to "make disciples of all nations, baptizing them" (Matt. 28:19). The church baptizes true converts in obedience to the Great Commission.

### *The Lord's Supper*

The Lord's Supper finds its roots in the Jewish Passover festival's commemoration of Israel's exodus from Egypt. Just before Jesus was betrayed and handed over to be crucified, he celebrated this "freedom meal" with his twelve disciples. In Jesus's mind, *he* was the fulfillment of Passover, the true sacrificial Lamb that ushers in a new and greater salvation. He instructed his disciples: "Do this in remembrance of me" (Luke 22:19).

---

35 Quoted in Stephen Neill, *A History of Christian Missions*, 2nd ed. (New York: Penguin, 1986), 378.

## CHAPTER I

Along with baptism, this meal marks out the church. It defines the boundary of who's "in" and who's "out." While baptism is the entry into the local church, the Lord's Supper is the regular, continuing snapshot of the church in good standing. Even in frontier missions settings, the Lord's Supper is a necessary celebration for every church.

Church fellowship centers around preaching and the Lord's Table (Acts 2:42; 20:7; Jude 12). Church discipline excludes an unrepentant sinner from the Lord's Table, that is, from membership. A Syrian pastor once told us, "That would never work in my culture." Of course, discipline is unpopular in every culture. But since the Lord's Supper is Jesus's family meal, only those in the family may participate (1 Cor. 11:27). Missions conferences, youth camps, small groups, weddings—none of these are appropriate venues for the Lord's Supper. This is because the Lord's Supper, along with baptism and true preaching, constitutes a church.

Missionaries today often overlook this meal. Even if local believers are gathering for worship and edification, the Lord's Supper is considered by some to be too "churchy," tainted by Western influence. Others set the ordinance aside because there's no recognized pastor to administer it. Missionaries remain in the background to promote indigenous leadership; meanwhile, Jesus's command to "do this in remembrance of me" is ignored.

But far from being bound to Western culture, the Lord's Supper was instituted by Jesus. Like baptism, the Lord's Supper is "inherently counter-cultural—requiring believers to publicly identify themselves with the culture of God's kingdom and stand out from the world."[36]

Both baptism and the Lord's Supper are central to the Great Commission. They're a "visible word" that portrays the gospel. This is why Paul writes that in the Lord's Supper "we proclaim the Lord's death until he comes" (1 Cor. 11:26). Such proclamation is central to the Great Commission.

### Singing

If you live in the Muslim world, every Friday you'll see men pouring into the mosques, reciting their prayers and going through their rituals. But one thing you won't hear or see is singing. There's no corporate praise in the mosque. There are no congregational hymns, no melodious praise, no instruments. W. M. Clow said, "Muslim worshippers never sing. . . . A Buddhist temple never resounds with a cry of praise. They are never jubilant with the songs of the forgiven."[37]

---

36 Vegas and Kocman, *Missions By the Book*, 69.

37 W. M. Clow, *The Cross in Christian Experience* (London: Houghton and Stodder, 1910), 278, quoted in John Stott, *The Cross of Christ* (Downer's Grove, IL: Intervarsity, 1986), 257.

## CHAPTER I

On the other hand, Christians can't seem to *stop* singing: in catacombs, in cathedrals, and everywhere throughout church history. In Saudi Arabia, the underground churches soundproof the walls and windows with mattresses so they can lift up their voices in praise.[38] "Make a joyful noise to the LORD, all the earth!" (Ps. 100:1).

After God's miraculous deliverance of his people from Egypt, they sang beside the Red Sea (Ex. 15:1). Today we enjoy an even greater deliverance, so Paul instructs churches to "be filled with the Spirit, addressing one another in psalms and hymns and spiritual songs, singing and making melody to the Lord with your heart" (Eph. 5:18–19).

Biblical singing doesn't require a building, a choir, or even instrumental accompaniment. For most of church history, singing was *a cappella*. Instruments can enhance the congregation's voices, but it must pass the "test of the catacombs,"

38 The worship venue matters. House churches are lower profile, while dedicated church buildings give visibility, long-term stability and legal sanction. See Benjamin Woodward, "The Benefits of Having a Building," 9Marks website, September 30, 2022, https://www.9marks.org/. In some parts of the world, worshiping in a home involves hospitality expectations that may not apply in an outside, dedicated building. "In Turkey, Islamic worship occurs in a dedicated religious meeting place and not the home. There is a high expectation of hospitality in the home—to ignore a guest in any way is offensive." Ken Caruthers, "The Missionary Team as Church: Applied Ecclesiology in the Life and Relationships Between Cross-Cultural Church Planters" (PhD diss., Southeastern Baptist Theological Seminary, 2014), 47.

the ancient burial caves where early persecuted Christians gathered to worship the risen Lord. If your worship can't be done there—if it needs dynamic lighting and smoke machines—then something is wrong.

Singing aligns our feelings with the sheer greatness of Christ and his gospel. Just as not even the whole world could contain all the books written of him (John 21:25), so not even all eternity will exhaust the songs of praise for him (Rev. 5:9). Through our singing, we anticipate the completion of the Great Commission.[39]

### *Biblical Leadership*

Nader was a young man from Egypt when he arrived at John's church in Dubai. He was affable and encouraging, and he naturally connected with the Arabic-speaking church members. As Nader got married and started raising a family, he developed a growing interest in missions and became the church's deacon of missions. Over time, people began to notice his shepherding gifts. He cared for the church's supported workers and checked in on them regularly. He began teaching more, and the congregation eventually recognized an elder who had grown up in their midst.

39 See John Folmar, "Why Christians Won't Stop Singing," The Gospel Coalition, September 15, 2024, https://www.thegospelcoalition.org/.

## CHAPTER I

Jesus Christ is the "head of the body, the church" (Col. 1:18), which he now rules from heaven. He has delegated authority to qualified leaders who care for his sheep. Scripture calls these men *elders*, *pastors*, or *overseers* (the three terms are used interchangeably in the New Testament). Elders teach (1 Tim. 3:2), protect (Titus 1:9), and set an example for the flock (1 Pet. 5:3). The other biblical office (deacon) exists to unify the body and promote gospel advancement through addressing tangible needs (1 Tim. 3:8). It's more about serving than shepherding.

Movement-driven missions considers the Bible largely silent on how churches should be led. Its proponents emphasize speed and measurable success. When it comes to leadership, they say, Christians are free to do whatever works or whatever culture dictates.

Nader had been a member of the church for seven years before he was installed as an elder. Training leaders takes time. It involves teaching and modeling and imitation (1 Cor. 11:1). That's why Paul said, "Do not be hasty in the laying on of hands" (1 Tim. 5:22). Parenting doesn't happen overnight, and neither does leadership development. Think farming rather than factory assembly. Qualified leaders develop over years, not months.

Training for Trainers (T4T) is an influential movement-driven methodology. It claims, "Each month, some 2,000 new

## WHAT IS THE CHURCH?

house churches and small groups are being started in villages, urban high-rises and factories."[40] Where do qualified leaders for these churches come from? Many are leaderless. In T4T, "You are free to develop new converts to lead. . . . In a new church situation, a new convert is not yet able to teach the Word, at least not eloquently."[41] This is despite Paul's warning that an elder "must not be a recent convert" (1 Tim. 3:6).[42]

It gets worse. Some missionaries say that to lead a house church one need not be a Christian at all. The Watsons write, "Did you know that lost people can evangelize? Well, they can

---

40 Smith, *T4T*, 36.

41 Smith, *T4T*, 270, 272.

42 T4T argues that 1 Timothy is addressing a mature church setting, but in a *new* church there is no such luxury. Paul's letter to Titus, they argue, drops the "recent convert" prohibition to account for a situation where there *are* no mature believers. T4T points to Acts 14:23, a situation where new churches were functioning before Paul and Barnabas "appointed elders for them in every church," to show that it is sometimes necessary for house churches to be led by new believers (Smith, *T4T*, 269–73). However, even in Titus, which may have been written to a newer church environment, an elder "must hold firm to the trustworthy word as taught, so that he may be able to give instruction in sound doctrine and also to rebuke those who contradict it" (Titus 1:9). Refuting error requires a knowledge of biblical doctrine. Far from setting a different standard, Titus 1:9 is an expansion of Paul's instruction to Timothy that the elder must be "apt to teach." As William Mounce said, "This spells out what Paul means when he tells Timothy that an overseer must be a 'skilled teacher.' (1 Tim 3:2)." Mounce, *Pastoral Epistles*, Word Biblical Commentary (Nashville: Thomas Nelson, 2000), 46:392.

## CHAPTER I

if you keep it simple enough."[43] Members of such churches are sheep without a shepherd, vulnerable to wolves.

Thankfully, the risen Lord gave "shepherds and teachers" to equip his churches for the work of the ministry (Eph. 4:11). For this equipping to happen, churches need biblical leaders who protect the sheep.

### A Pillar and Buttress of the Truth

In a desire for easily reproducible and rapidly multiplying churches, movement-driven missions has exchanged scriptural authority for a "best practices" approach. The paradigmatic question is simple: "Is this model of church something an average new believer can start and organize?"[44]

We should ask a different question: What does Scripture require?

The Bible offers guidance about how churches and missionaries should conduct themselves. Paul wrote to Timothy so that he might know "how one ought to behave in the household of God, which is the church of the living God"

---

43 Watson and Watson, *Contagious Disciple-Making*, 146. Former missionary Elliot Clark observed, in some cases, "missionaries encourage or expect *nonbelievers* to interpret, apply, obey, and teach the Bible apart from the indwelling Spirit." Clark, *Mission Affirmed*, 117n7.

44 Smith, *T4T*, 250.

(1 Tim. 3:15). God lives among his people, so it matters how we conduct ourselves in church. True churches are "God's household." He lives among them, especially in their public worship. Biblically qualified elders are crucial for the health of a church, which is "a pillar and buttress of the truth" (3:15). When believers sing and pray, when they hear the word read and preached, when baptism and the Lord's Supper are observed, there the Lord is especially present. As Mark Dever says, "Heaven appears on earth in God's assembly, the church."[45]

The local church is God's plan for the Great Commission—not missions agencies or parachurch ministries. On every continent and in every context, it's the local church that will ultimately *promote* and *protect* the truth of the gospel.

---

45 Mark Dever, *The Church: The Gospel Made Visible* (Wheaton, IL: Crossway, 2012), 5.

2

# What Is Missions?

When I (Scott) was about twelve years old, I entered Sunday school, and my friends were already talking about our visitors: missionaries from Africa. "Did you see the spiders?" "I tasted some of the candy they brought, and it was pretty good!" "They have pictures of themselves with lions and giraffes!"

There they were, at the front of the class: an older couple with gray hair that stood in stark contrast against their vibrant clothing. The man wore a bright blue shirt and blue pants; his wife wore a vivid red-and-white-striped floor-length skirt. In soft, kind voices, they introduced us to the objects on the table in front of them: wood-carved animals, musical instruments from their village, ceremonial bead necklaces, fly swatters made from animal hair and leather. What garnered the most *oohs* and *aahs* from us twelve-year-olds was the bug board:

## CHAPTER 2

the largest, grossest, scariest collection of bugs we could have ever imagined, pinned to a board in even rows.

These missionaries had our attention. We listened eagerly as they showed pictures of exotic animals and told stories of strange food (caterpillars, if I remember correctly). They told stories about teaching the gospel to whole villages of people.

I loved when missionaries visited our church! Even our parents seemed a little more interested than usual.

Several years later, my family joined a church whose pastor was a former missionary. We heard about missions all the time. I didn't really understand what it was, but I knew it had something to do with sharing the gospel with non-Christians in faraway lands. Though missions remained largely a mystery to me, what little I knew was enticing enough to make me want to know more. When I attended seminary, I made missions my major. I still remember the title of one of the first class lectures: "The Biblical Basis for Missions." Finally, I would learn what missions was all about!

The professor spent most of the class telling stories he would later tell us again. In the final ten minutes, he wrapped up by reading these expected verses:

And Jesus came and said to them, "All authority in heaven and on earth has been given to me. Go therefore and make disciples of all nations, baptizing them in the name of the Father and of the Son and of the Holy Spirit, teaching them to observe all that I have commanded you. And behold, I am with you always, to the end of the age." (Matt. 28:18–20)

Then he read another verse: "And this gospel of the kingdom will be proclaimed throughout the whole world as a testimony to all nations, and then the end will come" (Matt. 24:14). He closed his Bible and said simply, "We do the former in order to cause the latter—Christ's return."

Class dismissed.

Wait. Did I miss something? All the awe about missions I had as a child—the hushed tones and exciting presentations and special donations and sermon applications—all of it was based on only four verses that could be summarized in ten minutes?

Thankfully, the Bible has much more to say about missions, and what it has to say should guide us more than anything else. What is missions? Here's the answer that guides this series of books:

Missions involves churches sending qualified workers across linguistic, geographic, or cultural barriers to start

CHAPTER 2

or strengthen churches, especially in places where Christ has not been named.

Let's defend this definition by first reviewing key concepts from Scripture, then reflecting on the difficulties of defining missions, and finally unpacking our definition.

## Key Concepts from Scripture

In one sense, missions begins with Christ's final statements to his disciples between his resurrection and ascension. Each Gospel and the book of Acts contains a distinct moment where Jesus commissions his disciples for ministry.[1] Luke records two: one on the evening of Christ's resurrection (Luke 24:44–47), and one on the day of his ascension (Acts 1:8). As we look more closely at these two statements, however, we see that the foundation for missions had been laid long before.

After his resurrection, Jesus appeared to two of his disciples outside Jerusalem and then to the eleven and those gathered with them (Luke 24:33). He taught them about missions:

[1] Timothy C. Tennent, *Invitation to World Missions: A Trinitarian Missiology for the Twenty-First Century* (Grand Rapids, MI: Kregel Academic, 2010), chap. 5, "The Sending Father and the Sent Church." Tennent says we should think of the Great Commission as "a range of texts" where Jesus, after his resurrection, commissioned his disciples. Tennent includes Matthew 28:18–20; Mark 16:14–18; Luke 24:44–49; John 20:19–23; and Acts 1:7–8.

## WHAT IS MISSIONS?

Then he said to them, "These are my words that I spoke to you while I was still with you, that everything written about me in the Law of Moses and the Prophets and the Psalms must be fulfilled." Then he opened their minds to understand the Scriptures, and said to them, "Thus it is written, that the Christ should suffer and on the third day rise from the dead, and that repentance for the forgiveness of sins should be proclaimed in his name to all nations, beginning from Jerusalem. You are witnesses of these things. And behold, I am sending the promise of my Father upon you. But stay in the city until you are clothed with power from on high." (Luke 24:44–49)

Notice three truths from this passage that guide us in missions.

*First, God's word drives us forward.* "Everything written . . . must be fulfilled." Think back to the very beginning of creation. Worlds came into existence through divine words. Then God recorded more of his words in the pages of Scripture. Precisely because they are God's words, their fulfillment is certain (Luke 21:33). So it shouldn't surprise us that Jesus lived to fulfill God's word.[2]

---

2   There are more than thirty references in the gospels to a word or action "fulfilling" what had been written.

## CHAPTER 2

And yet, as God the Son, his own words are just as efficacious as his Father's. Even while fulfilling Old Testament prophecies, Jesus made his own prophetic statements. But though his disciples were surrounded by a river of prophetic words from the Father and the Son, they failed to understand. Until, that is, Jesus "opened their minds" (Luke 24:24). Only then did they understand that what God said about missions "must be fulfilled."

*Second, Jesus guarantees the victory.* Note that two of the three prophecies in Luke 24:46–47 had already happened:

1. Jesus's substitutionary death ("the Christ should suffer").
2. His victorious resurrection ("and on the third day rise from the dead").
3. Only one more remains to be fulfilled: "And that repentance for the forgiveness of sins should be proclaimed in his name to all nations."

This last event—the call for all nations to repent—is missions. It's still being fulfilled today. Its fulfillment began immediately after Christ's ascension. It's the focus of the book of Acts and the rest of the New Testament. Jesus's message to his disciples couldn't have been clearer: As surely as they witnessed him suffer on the cross and as surely as he was standing before them victorious over death following his resurrection, repentance for the forgiveness of sins in his name will be proclaimed to all nations.

*Finally, God finishes the task.* God loves fulfilling his word. The disciples will be the witnesses, but God is forever guiding the results. Luke's "Great Commission" is different from Matthew's (Matt 28:18–20). In Matthew, Jesus gives clear marching orders to "make disciples." In Luke, the only command is a curious one: "Stay in the city until you are clothed with power" (Luke 24:49). Jesus simply announces what will happen through the disciples.

God's commitment to accomplish missions according to his sovereign timing and power should encourage us on at least two levels. The Bible is the ongoing record of God's purposes failing in the hands of men but fulfilled by the power of God. So, first, we should be encouraged that God commits himself to the success of missions. Second, we should be encouraged that God still gives us an instrumental role to play (2 Cor. 5:17–20).

What we call missions today is the inevitable, ongoing, and Holy Spirit–empowered fulfillment of the call to all nations to repent and find forgiveness in Jesus Christ. When we let the Bible define missions, we'll guard against confusion and keep our missions practices on track.

CHAPTER 2

## Mission, Missions, and Missionaries:
## The Difficulty of Definitions

The term *missions* isn't in the Bible. Maybe this explains the lack of consensus on what the word actually means.

Should we define *mission*, *missions*, and *missionary*? Are all three necessary? Some missiologists use *mission* (singular) to refer to God's activities to restore goodness to his whole creation—in short, almost anything God does in the world.[3] Missiologists often use the term *missions* (plural) for specific activities of Christians as they obey God's mission-commands (in which case *missionaries* engage in specific *missions* as *mission*). Yep. It's all quite confusing.[4]

To further complicate matters, definitions of *missions* tend to focus on two lanes. There's the "broad mission," which refers to good works generally—digging wells, starting orphanages, and so on. And there's the "narrow mission," which refers specifically to evangelism, disciple making, and church planting.

We can't include everything a Christian does in our definition of *mission*. If we were to do so, we'd have to find yet an-

3  Kevin DeYoung and Greg Gilbert, *What Is the Mission of the Church?: Making Sense of Social Justice, Shalom, and the Great Commission* (Wheaton, IL: Crossway, 2011), 18.

4  See, for example, David J. Bosch, *Transforming Mission: Paradigm Shifts in Theology of Mission* (Maryknoll, NY: Orbis, 2011), 10.

other term to label the particular work of bringing the gospel to those who have never heard it. So what's our definition?

Missions involves churches sending qualified workers across linguistic, geographic, or cultural barriers to start or strengthen churches, especially in places where Christ has not been named.

Let's unpack this definition.

## Our Definition of Missions

### *Churches Sending Qualified Workers*

Missionaries can be the worst church members. Some believe their unique calling gives them a pass on ordinary church-manship. By neglecting to gather with other Christians (Heb. 10:24–25), they can set bad examples of what it means to follow Christ.

One national pastor friend had to ask Western missionaries, "Please, don't attend our church. I don't want our church members to learn your poor attendance habits." He told me with regret and shock that some missionaries in his city tried to recruit members away from his church to their own ministries. As I listened, embarrassed, to this African pastor's experiences, I wondered how the churches that sent and supported these missionaries would respond if someone were

## CHAPTER 2

to try these tactics in *their* neighborhood, with *their* church members.

Other missionaries I've encountered have never been baptized. They left their home countries in response to the Great Commission that calls them to baptize others, and yet baptism never hit their own to-do list.

I once attended a missionary training where the trainer had placed encouraging and inspiring quotes on the wall. One resonated with me: "Good leaders are found in the ranks of good followers." A decade later, while serving as a missions pastor in the United States, I began to wonder, "From what ranks are good missionaries found?"

Church members frequently have sought my counsel about their role in the Great Commission. These sweet brothers and sisters were determined to obey Christ even if it meant leaving all they knew to go to a place they'd never heard of. They come to me with simple questions: "What's my next step, pastor? How do I get ready for missionary service?"

How would you answer their questions? In the next chapter, we'll consider how sending churches equip and evaluate missionaries. But let's consider the missions agency for a moment.

When I led training for a large missionary sending agency, we received hundreds of applications every year. Each one

## WHAT IS MISSIONS?

included a statement from the candidate's church expressing support. And yet, at least one-third of all candidates had to delay because of documentable deficiencies in their personal discipleship. These shortcomings often came to light through the detailed questions of *our agency's interview process*. In other words, the sending churches had no idea there were any problems.

We received candidates from the ranks of "Christians who were excited about missions." But we needed more. We needed churches to reconsider their own missionary evaluation processes. After all, these same churches would never allow just any zealous church member to fill the office of deacon or elder. So why would they encourage such people to pursue missions?

As I write this chapter from an outside café, large commercial ships are navigating through the Bosphorus Strait that separates Europe and Asia. A quick Google search tells me that to perform this task one needs to meet a long list of qualifications: formal education in maritime studies or nautical science, naval certifications, experience navigating commercial ships, training in Bridge Resource Management, knowledge of local regulations, specific foreign language skills, and so on. Even with these qualifications, a seasoned captain still may not receive authorization to navigate these particular waters.

CHAPTER 2

Everywhere we look, we're surrounded by the need to meet certain qualifications before doing a certain job. These requirements aren't a hindrance to faithful service. They ensure it.

Why should missionary service be any different?[5] After all, the stakes are high. Imagine the disastrous effects of unqualified Christians starting churches and laying faulty doctrinal DNA among an unreached language group.

### *What's the Alternative?*

Over the last two hundred years, Christians have pressed the urgency of getting the gospel to the unreached. This urgency should increase preparation but sadly it leads churches to reduce it. It's as if the mindset were something like this: "If we wait too long, too many people will die without ever hearing the gospel."

Just imagine if captains drove their ships like that! In almost every area of life, we see the opposite. The need to get ships from the Marmara Sea into the Black Sea never leads commercial companies to drive their boats *quickly*. It leads them to drive them more *carefully*. Doctors and nurses don't rush through their preparation to get into the emergency room more quickly. No, as importance increases, preparation also increases.

5   Matt Rhodes, *No Shortcut to Success: A Manifesto for Modern Missions* (Wheaton, IL: Crossway, 2022), 27.

WHAT IS MISSIONS?

Preparing Christians according to the prescribed qualifications and processes in Scripture will certainly be slower. But it will also prevent the foolishness of sending members overseas who would never be allowed to serve in their own local churches.

### *Starting and Strengthening Churches*

In the Bible, churches sprang up wherever the gospel was preached. For example, Peter's proclamation of repentance and belief in the gospel at Pentecost resulted in thousands being baptized into Christ and added to the disciples. This group is called the church in Acts 5:11. When Paul persecuted the church in Acts 8, the scattered disciples proclaimed the gospel of Christ everywhere they went, so that new churches began to pop up all over Judea, Galilee, and Samaria (9:31).

Proclamation resulted in churches even in areas populated primarily by non-Jewish people. Traveling as far as Phoenicia, Cyprus, and Antioch, Christians proclaimed repentance for the forgiveness of sins, and many people believed in Christ. A regular gathering of disciples—a church—was birthed in Antioch (cf. Acts 11:26). God used Paul's sinful persecution of Christians to start a chain reaction that resulted in new churches!

When the church in Jerusalem heard of the new church in Antioch, they sent Barnabas to encourage them. Don't miss

## CHAPTER 2

the irony that Barnabas searched for Paul—now a Christian—to help him teach this new church and strengthen the disciples there (Acts 11:25). Paul and Barnabas were called to be church-strengtheners before they were sent by Antioch to be church-starters.

So when the Holy Spirit and the church in Antioch commissioned these qualified men for their work, Paul and Barnabas proclaimed the gospel throughout Cyprus and Galatia with predictable results. New churches sprang up. They bundled every harvest of disciples into organized communities so new Christians could live corporately the faith they believed individually. Retracing their steps before returning to Antioch, Paul and Barnabas strengthened these new churches with teaching (Acts 14:22–23). Their first missionary journey included both starting and strengthening churches.

Interestingly, the second journey began not with the idea of urgently getting the gospel to the lost but with strengthening the churches that had begun during the first journey. "Let us return and visit the brothers in every city where we proclaimed the word of the Lord, and see how they are" (Acts 15:36). This is exactly what Paul and Silas did after splitting with Barnabas and Mark (15:41). Of course, Paul and Silas also took the opportunity to proclaim the gospel in new places and start new churches along the way. In some cities, they remained a while "strengthening" new churches they had started (18:11). They rarely chose to leave but were instead forced out by hostile unbelievers. To others, they wrote letters or sent workers to encourage and strengthen (1 Thess. 2:17–3:5). In fact, the letters of the New Testament are the result of the apostles' strengthening ministry.

This is New Testament missions: proclaiming God's word to non-Christians in order to start new churches *and* teaching God's word to Christians to strengthen existing churches.

### *Not All "Missions" Is Missions*

I (Scott) took my first "missions" trip to Romania a few years after the Iron Curtain fell. Our small team partnered with a solid, Bible-preaching church in a poor city. We helped pour a concrete driveway for the church, visited a local orphanage with gifts for sick children, and bought a horse for a church member (against the advice of our host). We sang and played musical instruments during the church's worship services and "taught" sermonettes to the eager Christians. We were pretty good at the music, but no one on our team had any biblical training or qualifications to teach the Bible. Looking back on it now, what we provided more than anything was our wealth as Westerners and our zeal as young people. We did a lot of good. We were generous, caring, and servant hearted.

## CHAPTER 2

We looked after the poor and the orphans—all activities the Bible directs Christians to do.

But we weren't doing "missions." Our priority wasn't to start new churches or to strengthen the church we served. Sure, we did everything in the name of Christ. But mostly, we engaged in service projects. Again, all good things—but not the greatest need of our world, and not the priority we see in the New Testament. Our trip was "ministry" not "missions."

"Missions" is not anything a Christian does with a passport in the pocket, or any good deed done in the name of Christ while in another country. It's not even simply evangelism or making disciples or baptizing. Missions involves starting churches as we proclaim Christ (evangelism) in order to baptize new Christians into a church that will teach them to obey all that Christ commanded.

So what's the place of good deeds? They "adorn" the gospel (Titus 2:10); they don't replace it. As Greg Gilbert and Kevin DeYoung write, "We believe the church is sent into the world to witness to Jesus by proclaiming the gospel and making disciples of all nations. This is our task. This is our unique and central calling."[6] When good deeds eclipse the priority of proclamation, we've lost the plot.

6  DeYoung and Gilbert, *What Is the Mission of the Church?*, 26.

### *Across Barriers*

Missions involves crossing linguistic, geographic, or cultural barriers.

Winston Churchill is often credited with saying, "British and Americans are two people separated by a common language." Though we speak the same language, our different accents can be indecipherable. How much more the barrier between, say, English and Turkish!

At Pentecost, God supernaturally overcame the stubborn barrier of *language*. As a result, three thousand Jews who were from many nations and spoke many different tongues were added to the church (Acts 2:11, 41). From there, the news of Christ's death and resurrection carried throughout the streets and neighborhoods of Jerusalem. Then these new Christ followers carried the gospel with them when they went home to the surrounding villages and provinces of Judea.

Language barriers arguably remain the most significant barrier for church planting and effective evangelism. The apostle Paul himself admits as much: "If I do not know the meaning of the language, I will be a foreigner to the speaker and the speaker a foreigner to me" (1 Cor. 14:11). In this passage, Paul encourages the Corinthian Christians that intelligible teaching of the message of Christ should take priority

## CHAPTER 2

over supernatural demonstrations of the Holy Spirit, like the ability to speak in unknown tongues. The principle remains and can shape our missions work. Our ministries will be ineffective unless we speak the gospel to people in a language our hearers can understand.

For this reason, the foundational work of missions will continue to be Christian witnesses doing the difficult work of learning foreign languages in order to teach the whole counsel of Scripture effectively.

The importance of language explains why pioneer missionary Henry Martyn went to such lengths to translate God's word. Martyn was a celebrated Cambridge scholar who left England at the age of twenty-five, leaving behind the woman he hoped one day to marry. He went to India, and later Persia, where he translated Scripture into foreign languages. Confronted by Hindu idolatry in India, Martyn was shaken. "I shivered at being in the neighborhood of hell; my heart was ready to burst at the dreadful state to which the devil had brought my poor fellow creatures. I would have given the world to have known the language, to have preached to them."[7]

Imagine the difficulty—without Google Translate or any modern language center—of traveling alone to India and

7   Richard T. France, "Henry Martyn" in *Five Pioneer Missionaries* (Edinburgh, UK: Banner of Truth, 1965), 265.

## WHAT IS MISSIONS?

learning Hindustani and later Persian. What motivated Martyn? One biographer said, "The man who slaved away his life among people whom the lowest clerk of the East India Company despised, and who dragged his dying body over many hundreds of miles of sea and mountains, did it for this purpose: to save men and women from destruction."[8]

The gospel also overcame *cultural* barriers. Everywhere the first disciples traveled, whether in Israel or throughout the Roman Empire, they encountered people who hadn't heard of Christ. Philip went to Samaria. Peter witnessed to the Gentiles. Because Koine Greek was a common trade language, many disciples were able to cross cultural barriers without ever needing to learn a new language.

The gospel also overcame *geographic barriers*, as when the church in Antioch sent Paul and Barnabas on long journeys deep into Asia Minor and Macedonia.

With each barrier they crossed, the apostles spread the news of Christ and established churches. This is what Christians have always done: They take the gospel across linguistic, cultural, and geographic barriers so that Christ's fame can fill the earth.

Church history has followed the apostles' example. In the twelfth century, Raymond Lull founded a missionary training

8   France, *Five Pioneer Missionaries*, 301.

CHAPTER 2

school to teach foreign languages so that Christians could carry the gospel to faraway people. Over the centuries, the missions task came into sharper focus. As the knowledge of Christ spread throughout the world, Christians discovered new barriers to cross for the sake of the gospel. Today, thanks to many Christians' tireless work, there are communities of believers in almost every country of the world. And yet, significant barriers remain.

In 1974, at the Congress for World Evangelization in Lausanne, Switzerland, global missions strategy shifted from a focus on gospel work in countries to a focus on gospel work among "people groups." *People groups* came to be defined as "the largest group within which the gospel can spread as a church planting movement without encountering barriers of understanding or acceptance."[9] In 1995, the Joshua Project began as a research initiative to bring attention to "unreached peoples." As a result, churches began to focus their missions efforts among those groups.[10]

9   Joshua Project, "People Group, Definitions," Joshua Project, http://www.joshua project.net/help/definitions/, accessed October 17, 2024.
10  The Joshua Project formally defines a people group as "unreached" if their population includes "less than or equal to 5% Christian Adherent and less than or equal to 2% Evangelical." By "Christian adherent," they mean anyone who identifies as Christian—including many whom Protestant Christians would say are not. By "evangelical," they mean those who "align themselves with churches

76

## WHAT IS MISSIONS?

We're thankful for the Joshua Project and the focus it has brought to reaching the unreached. But the results are complicated: The organization doesn't try to count actual conversions or churches. According to the Bible, missions is more than simply moving all people groups, one by one, from the "unreached" column to the "reached" column—whatever that means. And, really, what does "reached" mean? Rather, the Great Commission is a call to make disciples of *all* the nations (Matt. 28:19). For this reason, churches must pray for and determine how to work for the progress of the gospel in *both* their hometown (localized church ministry) *and* among people and places where Christ is not known (missions).

Both are important. If we say, "Gospel work is for everywhere, including my hometown," then we might never go to the unreached because we might think doing ministry nearby will satisfy the missions mandate of Scripture. But if we say, "Gospel ministry is only for the unreached," then

---

where the gospel is being proclaimed" whether or not they themselves have experienced genuine conversion. In other words, Joshua Project data does not count converted Christians. According to the Joshua Project, over 40 percent of the world's total population fits their classification of "unreached." See "Joshua Project—Definitions and Terms Related to the Great Commission," accessed April 15, 2024, http://www.joshuaproject.net/help/definitions/. "In many nations only 10–40% of Evangelicals so defined may have had a valid conversion and also regularly attend church services."

## CHAPTER 2

we might discourage Christians from *also* ministering in their hometowns. We should resist simplistic, all-or-nothing definitions. The Bible shows that God will settle for nothing less than the spread of Christ's fame in "all" places—near and far. Church members must pray for the spread of the gospel among "all" nations.

These remain the main significant barriers missionaries cross today for gospel work among "all nations": geographic, cultural, and especially linguistic.

### Where Christ Has Not Been Named

When qualified missionaries are backed by their church, ready to cross significant barriers for the gospel, and are committed to starting and strengthening churches, how should they think about where to minister?

Even the most prepared individuals can make mistakes. In 2010, hand surgeon David Ring successfully operated to treat the carpal tunnel syndrome in a patient's left hand. The only problem? She wasn't suffering from carpal tunnel syndrome but from a "stuck" ring finger. Fifteen minutes after the procedure, the doctor realized he had performed the wrong surgery. He quickly and humbly confessed his mistake to the patient and offered to perform the correct procedure if she were willing. She was, and the second surgery went perfectly.

## WHAT IS MISSIONS?

Understandably, she declined to have Dr. Ring involved in her follow-up care; she had lost faith in him. After all, he had performed surgery on the healthy part of her hand.[11]

Does anything like this ever happen in missions? Do we send precious resources to otherwise healthy locations?

The apostle Paul always seemed to consider where Christ still needed to receive glory. Paul said, "From Jerusalem and all the way around to Illyricum I have fulfilled the ministry of the gospel of Christ; and thus I make it my ambition to preach the gospel, not where Christ has already been named, lest I build on someone else's foundation" (Rom. 15:19–20). Having left churches in these locations, he was confident that they could continue the ministry that was necessary there— the ongoing witness for Christ in those regions. Instead, Paul was thinking of places that had no churches, where Christ had not been named; that's where he would go next. He concluded, "But now, since I no longer have any room for work in these regions, and since I have longed for many years to come to you, I hope to see you in passing as I go to Spain" (15:23–24). The apostle Paul prioritized people who had no witness for Christ. We should at least consider that need even as we see genuine, ongoing needs in other places.

[11] Scott Hensley, "A Surgeon Confesses to Error and Hopes It's a Lesson Learned," NPR, November 12, 2010, https://www.npr.org/.

## CHAPTER 2

Missions in our day is full of great-hearted Christians who, full of compassion, long to help those who are suffering in the world by telling them of the love of Jesus. There is so much to commend in that spirit! However, even the best surgeons can mistakenly operate where it is not needed.

Before any missions endeavor, whether short- or long-term, everyone involved in the planning should first consider whether the work they are planning to do is actually needed. Before sending resources to do evangelism, first reach out to the believers who actually live in that place and ask if you should. When you pray about starting a church in a city, find out from the churches that are already there if that's the best course of action.

You might be surprised to hear that even though a city might have a healthy church or two, much work might remain. For example, has the Bible been fully translated into the local language? Are national Christians evangelizing much? Is there a network of healthy churches? Are there ways to train up pastors? Do new pastors have access to theological education? Do believers have worship music they can use to praise God with in their gatherings? Do national Christians have access to Christian literature in their language? These are all great needs in many places of the world where there are national Christians and churches.

WHAT IS MISSIONS?

Most of all, verify that what you see as a need is valid—especially with the believers who live there. A genuine need should be recognized by more than just sincere but faraway Christians. When churches on the ground agree with you, the need you are addressing becomes a verified, recognized need by Christians whom God has providentially raised up in that place. Partnering with Christians on the ground will go a long way to build relationships and ensure help and support as you minister.

## Conclusion

Who would have suspected that God would use a bug board from visiting African missionaries to capture a twelve-year-old's heart toward missions? Certainly not me.

After my wife and I married, the pastor of our church in Virginia where I served on staff strongly encouraged us to pursue missions ministry. So we headed off to seminary to receive more focused training. After seminary, we were evaluated by our church and deemed qualified to go. We joined a missions agency that would (a) prepare us to cross significant barriers, most notably linguistic, in order to (b) start and strengthen churches in (c) places of high need, where Christ had not been named. I am thankful for those days and for the godly men and women who helped prepare us. I am most

## CHAPTER 2

thankful for those who passed on to us a reverence and awe and a passion and love for Christ's bride, the church.

On recruitment day, a brother who had served in Africa almost convinced me to join his team instead. But when he heard where we were headed, he changed his mind. "Keep on the path, brother," he said. "Where you are going has more need of churches than where we are."

Our team landed in Central Asia as five adults and four babies—with lots of ideas and zero experience. Thankfully, our preparations had emphasized that we should always cling to God's word and work to start churches as the goal of missions. Those were the pillars of our work.

We gave ourselves to language study. It was my full-time job for a year. Cyndi kept at it until she reached a critical level of proficiency. As soon as we could adequately communicate gospel truths and determine when we had made language errors while teaching Bible doctrine, we threw ourselves into Bible study with any who would join us.

Within one year, God gave us the first convert in our city. Then more were interested to study. Soon, we had a handful of friends who met regularly to learn God's word. When we had several professing Christians, we organized as a church and baptized them. They were as eager to become a part of the church as we were to incorporate them, since we had been

82

reading about "church" again and again in Scripture. "That's us!" they would say.

From there, we settled into a rhythm of church life that lasted several years. We focused on the "one another" commands of Scripture (we regularly repeated, "We take ownership for one another"), discipleship growth in holy living, and understanding the gospel better. When Cyndi and I eventually left, we left behind a church with local believers.

Our time in Central Asia taught me two great truths: Christ is a mighty Savior, and God can establish churches in even the darkest places of our planet.

3

# Church as the Origin of Missions

Margaret had been a Christian for two years when a sending agency commissioned her as a missionary to Jordan. She had never been a member of a church. In fact, she had rarely attended one, and she had no relationship with any pastor. She hung out at a Christian-owned coffee shop and considered that to be her community. She was unaware she needed a church.

After her conversion, she attended a discipleship training school where she was taught to share the gospel and mobilize others for the Great Commission. During trainings in Hawaii, people got together for worship but "church was optional." Margaret recalled, "It was a super-individualized approach

## CHAPTER 3

to the Christian life." Shortly thereafter, agency leaders laid hands on her and sent her to Jordan with no oversight of a local church.

After a few months on the field, Margaret resigned. Her field leaders supported the teaching that belief in the divinity of Christ was not necessary for salvation. She knew that was wrong.

She wrote to her leaders: "My concern is that with these loose boundaries we are creating nominal Christians who aren't truly regenerate and don't know the true gospel." Leadership replied, "We do not have a written statement about what we believe regarding the doctrine of salvation. We purposely never wrote a 'Statement of Faith' because we are an international movement of Christians from many denominations."

Margaret agonized over what to do. Should she continue to partner with team members who did not believe that the deity of Christ is essential for salvation?[1] She needed help. She

---

1 See Matt Rhodes, "For the Joy Set Before Us," unedited manuscript (Wheaton, IL: Crossway, forthcoming). In his book, Matt Rhodes has discussed his concern that "missions methods often neglect to mention Christ's divinity to Muslims in the process of evangelism. Indeed, it's not unusual for his divinity to be largely glossed over through follow-up discipleship programs designed to help new believers plant new churches." Why omit such a central truth of the gospel? Rhodes says it is because "so many missionaries are trained to present the gospel in ways that fail to highlight the exclusive claims of Christ or those that hearers might find offensive."

## CHURCH AS THE ORIGIN OF MISSIONS

needed a pastor. She needed a church. But Margaret had to make the decision by herself. She decided to go back home and, through a friend, began attending a faithful church.

If she had been a member of a healthy church before launching into cross-cultural missions, she would have felt more supported and accountable on the field. Perhaps most importantly, she would have had help when she faced conflict and confusion.

Contrast Margaret's situation with one from fifty years earlier. In 1973, Joseph wanted to be a "tentmaker." He wanted to live in an Arabian city as a petroleum chemist in the oil and gas industry and share the gospel. He sought advice from a seasoned veteran on the field. The experienced missionary said, "It appears you have a lot of drive and energy for the execution of physical tasks. As a Christian brother, though, I'd caution you strongly against entering the ministry of the gospel without a home church behind you 100 percent."

Some evangelists in the Muslim world had been deported. Others had become disillusioned and given up. For missionaries to endure, they needed the prayers and encouragement of a sending church. The missionary told Joseph, "I think it is of utmost importance that you cultivate an intimate relationship with a local church which will feel entirely behind you and responsible for you." According to this missionary, the

CHAPTER 3

church fuels the ministry. He warned Joseph not to work as a "loner."[2]

Too often, missions agencies ignore the church when considering a missionary's qualifications. Individuals are told that the decision is "between the missionary and his or her God." But missionaries are "sent ones," and the church—under God—is the sender. As the Southgate Fellowship affirms, "Because mission belongs to Christ and Christ is head of his church, the visible church is his chosen agent responsible for sending out gifted and godly men and women to call people to repentance and faith."[3]

## Church-Centered Sending

In the New Testament, the local church is the origin of missionary activity. The church at Antioch launched the first missionary endeavor among the Gentile nations. As the church gathered to worship the Lord, the Holy Spirit said, "Set apart for me Barnabas and Saul for the work to which I have called them" (Acts 13:2). The Lord of the harvest initiated the effort, but not apart from a local church: "Then after

2  Unpublished correspondence from Leon Blosser to Joseph O'Hanlon Jr., March 9, 1973.

3  The Southgate Fellowship, "Affirmations and Denials Concerning World Mission," *Themelios* 45, no. 1 (April 2020): 125. Available at https://thesouthgatefellowship.org/.

88

## CHURCH AS THE ORIGIN OF MISSIONS

fasting and praying they laid their hands on them and sent them off" (13:3).

At the end of their first journey, Paul and Barnabas returned to their sending church in Antioch: "And when they arrived and gathered the church together, they declared all that God had done with them, and how he had opened a door of faith to the Gentiles. And they remained no little time with the disciples" (Acts 14:27–28). They had been commissioned and sent, and now they reported back to the church and were refreshed.[4]

For decades, missions organizations have pooled resources and expertise to make valuable contributions to the global cause. But the local church remains the engine behind Great Commission work. As Andy Johnson put it, "Any humanly-invented organization that assists in missions must remember that they are a bridesmaid, not the bride. They are stage-hands, not the star."[5]

I (John) went to the Evangelical Christian Church of Dubai (ECCD) in 2005.[6] I'll never forget the loving support of my

---

4 Note Paul's continued association with the Antioch church in Acts 15:35 and 18:22. The same pattern appears in 3 John 6, where missionaries, upon returning from the field, "testified before the church." Other churches (such as Berea, Thessalonica, and Derbe) vetted, approved, and sent out workers (Acts 20:4). Paul called such workers "messengers of the churches, the glory of Christ" (2 Cor. 8:23).

5 Andy Johnson, *Missions: How the Local Church Goes Global* (Wheaton, IL: Crossway, 2017), 27.

6 Portions of this chapter are from John Folmar, "Send Missionaries and Inspire Senders," *9Marks Journal*, June 30, 2020, https://www.9marks.org/.

sending church (Capitol Hill Baptist Church in Washington, DC). The members prayed and even helped me box up my books. They hand-wrote messages on the boxes: "May the word of the Lord speed ahead and be honored." I have benefited from the long-term, sacrificial commitment of a sending church that has prayed for us and backed us from afar.

Now my church in Dubai is a sender. We're charged to equip new leaders who will entrust the gospel to others (2 Tim. 2:2), not only locally but further afield. Through our pastoral internship, we've trained and sent indigenous pastors who are now serving churches in Morocco, Libya, Egypt, Jordan, Kazakhstan, India, Nepal, Indonesia, Japan, the UAE, and beyond.

A sending church must bear in mind its responsibilities for missionaries both before they go and after they have gone.

## Before They Go

The most important missionary training doesn't occur in seminary or at a missions agency's training center. It occurs during years of membership in a healthy church.

Missionaries are equipped through the ordinary work of the church, which includes the following.

*Expositional Preaching.* An occasional topical missions sermon may be inspiring. Hosting a global missions week can be informative. But neither of these prepares a heart like the long-term commitment to expositional preaching. My own interest in missions began to grow as I regularly sat under preaching that emphasized the glory of God and the world-wide purposes of the gospel.

*Meaningful membership.* Church isn't an event we attend; it's a family we join. Meaningful membership carries both privileges and responsibilities. It formalizes the kind of Spirit-wrought fellowship and accountability that would-be missionaries should aspire to replicate on the field.

*Discipling.* The apostle Paul said, "Be imitators of me, as I am of Christ" (1 Cor. 11:1). Discipling involves a chain of imitation: Jesus → Paul → Timothy → others. It involves not only sound doctrine but a way of life. Such imitation is "deeply and inescapably relational," and it's caught as much as it's taught.[7] How many missionaries on the field have never been discipled?

*Worship.* "Before a man is a missionary he must be a Christian."[8] If worship is a reflex-response to greatness, and if a Christian is one who has seen the splendor of God's glory in the face of Jesus Christ (2 Cor. 4:6), then a prerequisite

7  Colin Marshall and Tony Payne, *The Trellis and the Vine: The Ministry Mindshift that Changes Everything* (Kingsford, Australia: Matthias Media, 2009), 71.

8  Tom Wells, *A Vision for Missions* (Edinburgh, UK: Banner of Truth, 1985), 22.

for a missionary is to be captivated by God's glory in Christ. The missionary's job description is to "declare his glory among the nations" (Ps. 96:3). We cannot declare what we have not experienced.

Missions-centered churches send church-centered missionaries who are not only converted but biblically qualified.

### *Make Sure Your Missionaries Are Christians*

Assuming that missionaries believe the gospel could have disastrous effects.

Jeff and Sally and their boys went to Bolivia with the missionary organization of their mainline US denomination. They had grown up in unhealthy churches, but a humanitarian impulse led them to become missionaries in South America. Their mission board taught them to raise funds. "There was never any expectation to evangelize," they said. "They had local pastors there to handle that." For five years, Jeff and Sally lived in Bolivia, running an agricultural center and a school.

As the years passed and ministry pressure mounted, their marriage began to suffer. They were burned out from constant infighting and corruption. Looking for help, Sally discovered something new through the internet—biblical teaching and sound doctrine. She shared it with Jeff. "It captured our attention and hearts," she said, "and we knew it was time to leave the denomination we had both grown up in."

They left the mission field—dejected—and began attending an evangelical church. During the new members' class, a pastor explained the gospel clearly. That day, they realized something shocking: "We had been missionaries in Bolivia but we weren't genuine Christians." In time, they both repented and believed.

Jeff and Sally weren't the first unconverted missionaries. Almost three centuries before, John Wesley journeyed from England to the Georgia colony. After his return to England in 1738, he exclaimed, "I went to America to convert the Indians; but oh, who shall convert me?"[9]

Assuming the gospel in the sending process only harms the cause and the missionary. How can one give what he does not have?

### *Assess Your Missionaries*

Evaluating missionary candidates is a weighty responsibility. How much damage on the mission field has occurred because churches were unwilling to deny well-intentioned but unqualified candidates? How many individuals have

9 Arnold Dallimore, *George Whitefield: The Life and Times of the Great Evangelist of the Eighteenth-Century Revival* (Edinburgh, UK: Banner of Truth, 1970), 1:150.

## CHAPTER 3

been demoralized trying to fill a role for which they were unqualified?

Healthy churches both equip and assess missionary candidates. Sending churches must discern candidates' levels of *conviction*, *competence*, and *character*.[10]

*Conviction.* Do the missionary candidates:

- wholeheartedly agree with the sending church's statement of faith?
- believe in the inerrancy of Scripture and the exclusivity of Christ?
- have a doctrine of God that is sufficient for cross-cultural ministry (including an understanding of the Trinity, God's attributes, and God's sovereignty)?
- understand the importance of the local church and biblical ecclesiology?
- show an ability to evaluate current trends in missions (e.g., Insider Movement, Church Planting Movements, Four Fields, Disciple Making Movements)?

*Competence.* Since missions involves proclamation, can the candidates clearly teach gospel truth? Are they already doing

10 These "three C's" are borrowed from the training approach of Marshall and Payne, *Trellis and the Vine*, 78.

## CHURCH AS THE ORIGIN OF MISSIONS

locally the ministry they want to do overseas? Do they have track records of fruitfulness in teaching, discipling, and evangelism? Have people grown spiritually under their ministries?

*Character.* Do they meet the criteria of 1 Timothy 3:1–13? (These criteria apply for female missionaries as well as men, although women's roles on the field will differ from men's.) Are they known and respected in the congregation? Why are they pursuing missions? Are they really going out "for the sake of the name" (3 John 7)? Or does some other reason animate them (such as idealism, ambition, or guilt)? Examining his own motives, Robert Murray M'Cheyne recorded in his diary, "Why is a missionary life so often an object of my thoughts? Is it simply for the love I bear for souls? Then, why do I not show it more where I am? Souls are as precious here as in Burma."[11]

A missionary to Niger once described the common mindset among missions agencies: "If you love Jesus, you can go." That was it. But that's not enough. A missionary must be equipped and assessed by his or her church. Other factors may be worth considering too: physical health, strength of marriage, contentment in singleness, capacity to learn a new

---

11 Andrew Bonar, *Robert Murray M'Cheyne* (Edinburgh, UK: Banner of Truth, 1960), 29. He added: "Does the romance of the business not weigh anything with me?—the interest and esteem I would carry with me?—the nice journals and letters I would write and receive? . . . Am I wholly deceiving my own heart?" (29).

language and operate in a cross-cultural environment, an ability to hold down a job, and so on.[12] But merely feeling "passionate" is not enough.

In evaluating their gifts, Paul urged the Romans to "think with sober judgment" (Rom 12:3). This happens best in a faithful church, where a man or woman is known.[13]

### Send Your Best

In Acts 13, the Holy Spirit directed the church at Antioch to "set apart" Barnabas and Paul for missions outreach. Imagine losing two leaders of that caliber! Yet Antioch was willing to pay the price.

I can testify to how difficult it is to send beloved church members. In 2010, our church sent more than one hundred kingdom-minded members—including multiple staff, an

---

12  Matt Rhodes, *No Shortcut to Success* (Wheaton, IL: Crossway, 2022), 217.

13  In some cases, missions committees are asked to support missionaries unconnected to the church. Take all deliberate care in the assessment process. Get to know the candidate's doctrine and ministry. Spend time with the candidate and get reliable character assessments. Better to invest heavily in a few trusted partners than support many missionaries whose character you don't know. See Elliot Clark's "Questions for the Prospective Missionary," in *Mission Affirmed: Recovering the Missionary Motivation of Paul* (Wheaton, IL: Crossway, 2022), 234. Heed Andy Johnson's caution: "If a worker is offended that you want to explore the contours of his or her theology, that should be a huge red flag." *Missions: How the Local Church Goes Global* (Wheaton, IL: Crossway, 2017), 65.

elder, and deacons—to start a new church on the other side of town. There was an exodus of friendship, energy, ministry, and finances. The church planters had embarked on an exciting mission for God; we were left holding the bag, with empty seats, a stripped-down music team, and missing leaders. It was costly and painful.

But over time, as we slowly grew back, we realized that a multiplication of ministry had occurred. The new church was bearing witness on the other side of town and reaching a different community. And we grew spiritually as a result—we enjoyed stronger unity and deepened faith as we saw the Lord provide for us through new leaders. Our congregational singing even grew stronger because we had to compensate for the lost musicians! We'd exported many of our most enterprising, faithful members, but somehow we were the ones who were blessed.

Whether Antioch then or our churches now, we must be prepared to send out our best.

### *Decide on a Sending Agency*

Missions agencies and field partners possess more know-how and experience than many local churches. They help in technical areas like cross-cultural training, language learning, computer security, missionary health, and evacuation. For this reason, churches shouldn't try to "run the show" from the other

CHAPTER 3

side of the world. Matt Rhodes cautions, "Sending churches should tread carefully—especially where they don't understand the cultural practicalities and pressures of missionary life."[14] Good agencies understand the variables of culture and context. At their best, they're valuable partners, especially in difficult locations.

However, two problems often arise in the relationship between churches and sending agencies.

1. Churches delegate their God-given responsibilities to others. They hand over the reins to the "experts" and fail to give meaningful oversight. Perhaps they believe themselves to be unqualified to provide oversight. Or perhaps they deny that the local church remains responsible for a missionary's theological and methodological faithfulness.[15]

2. Not all missions agencies promote helpful missions. Sometimes, "partnership" with agencies means platforming a watered-down approach to missions. Walt Chantry criticized some independent agencies: "Mission boards are hesitant to answer the question, 'What is the gospel?' To answer that thoroughly would condemn what many of their

---

14 Matt Rhodes, "Book Review: *Mission Affirmed*, by Elliot Clark," 9Marks website, August 4, 2022, https://www.9marks.org/.

15 "We deny that denominational agencies and parachurch organizations should have the primary theological, moral, and ministry-method oversight of missionaries." Southgate Fellowship, "Affirmations and Denials," 126.

own missionaries preach. It would destroy the mission society, which is a federation of churches who have differing answers to that question."[16] This is what Margaret faced in Jordan.

Theological misalignment between sending churches and missions agencies undermines church planting. Missionaries shouldn't spend their time battling over theology and strategy. There's too much work to be done.

Brooks Buser, president of Radius International, noted areas a church should investigate before deciding on a missions agency:[17]

1. How does the agency value language fluency? How should language acquisition affect ministry the first two or three years on the field?

2. What is the agency's definition of a church? What role should the local church play on the field?

3. What is its understanding of conversion? Should professing converts be individually screened before being baptized?

4. How does the agency understand contextualization? Is it permissible for new believers to continue worshiping in mosques and identifying as "Muslim" followers of Jesus?

---

16  Walter Chantry, *Today's Gospel: Authentic or Synthetic?* (Edinburgh, UK: Banner of Truth, 1970), 3.

17  A. Sequeira, B. Buser, J. Mack Stiles, J. Leeman, and S. Logsdon, "On Church-Centered Missions vs. Movement-Driven Missions," 9Marks Pastors Talk, October 12, 2021, https://www.9marks.org/.

5. What is its position on missions methods and techniques such as "obedience-based discipleship," "Discovery Bible studies," and "Person of Peace"?

6. Is the agency a "big tent" organization that allows a diversity of viewpoints and philosophies? Or is it a "top-down" organization that dictates acceptable methods and strategies?

Sending agencies can be helpful catalysts. But they can also hinder good missions work. Sending-church leaders need to discern the difference.

### *Become Talent Scouts*

For forty years, gospel work has flourished among Reformed Baptist congregations of Lusaka, Zambia. Over the decades, Kabwata Baptist Church has planted more than forty congregations. Their outreach has extended from the Baptist churches of Lusaka into Botswana, Malawi, Namibia, Nigeria, Rwanda, Sierra Leone, Tanzania, and Zimbabwe.

Kabwata's pastor, Conrad Mbewe, writes, "It is the responsibility of church leaders to prayerfully identify those whom God is calling to this all-important work and to send them off."[18] Sometimes this means recruiting qualified

18  Conrad Mbewe, *God's Design for the Church: A Guide for African Pastors and Ministry Leaders* (Wheaton, IL: Crossway, 2020), 157.

candidates from the outside and appointing them as leaders of a new work. More often, it involves recognizing qualified leaders the Lord has already raised up. Two Australian church leaders describe it like this: "We should be talent scouts . . . constantly on the lookout for the sort of people with the gifts and integrity to preach the word and pastor God's people."[19]

In Dubai, we've "rerouted" several church members into missions and church-planting work, including:

- a former physical therapist who now pastors an English-language church in the UAE;
- a former school tutor who now pastors a Russian-language church in Almaty, Kazakhstan;
- a former engineer who now pastors a German-language church in Munich;
- a former sales associate who now pastors a Nepali congregation in Kathmandu;
- a former security guard who now pastors a new Hindi church plant in Bihar, India; and
- a former honey-sales entrepreneur who aspires to pastor an Arabic-language church in the region.

19  Marshall and Payne, *Trellis and the Vine*, 139. See also pages 141–42 for a helpful list of qualities and characteristics that identify "people worth watching."

CHAPTER 3

These were all fruitful members of our English-language church. They'd moved to Dubai for work. But over time, they began to demonstrate ministerial gifting—a hunger for divine truth, a love for God's people, an ability to teach, and a positive spiritual impact on both church members and non-Christians. So we trained and redeployed them.[20]

### *Establish Ecclesiology*

A missionary's ministry DNA is established before he ever gets on the field. His understanding of church, his personal experience of the sanctifying power of a unified congregation, his appreciation of a culture of evangelism—these things are set in place long before his agency's "sending celebration."

Ali, a Moroccan underground house-church pastor, was frustrated. Simo, a promising new believer who had grown up in an orphanage, was a member of his church. After Simo

20 John Folmar, "Raise Up Leaders," 9Marks website, June 10, 2024, https://www .9marks.org/. Local, indigenous leadership is key for gospel penetration in underreached areas of the world. By virtue of their geographic location, churches on the missions field, including English-language international churches, have a unique opportunity to reach and train promising leaders from those gospel-needy cultures. As William Carey concluded, "It is only by means of native preachers that we can hope for the universal spread of the gospel throughout this immense continent. Europeans are too few, and their subsistence costs too much, for us ever to hope that they can possibly be the instruments" for the cause of the gospel in India. "Serampore Form of Agreement," para. 8 (1805).

came to faith, the church cared for him in practical ways. Members taught him to play guitar, and he became one of the church's song leaders. Simo regularly said of the church, "They are my family."

When an American missionary came to Ali offering to help, Ali asked him to give Simo a job. After working at the missionary's dental supply company, Simo told the church he would be leaving them to join the American's home group (they needed a song leader). The church was devastated. Simo later admitted that finances were the main reason for his departure. His loyalty had shifted to his employer. To beef up his own ministry, the missionary had harmed the indigenous church.

Ali laments that such interference is not uncommon. At their regular associational meetings, indigenous Moroccan pastors have discussed the mixed influence of foreign missionaries. One pastor lamented, "When missionaries visit the church, later it splits." Another national pastor (in northern India) expressed similar caution: "Please don't send bad workers. If a person cannot be an elder in your church, then don't send them. . . . We don't want mavericks. We don't want entrepreneurs. We don't want go-getters."[21]

---

21  Harshit Singh, "How Western Methods Have Affected Missions in India," 9 Marks' First Five Years Conference, Columbus, OH, August 4, 2017, quoted in Rhodes, *No Shortcut to Success*, 205.

## CHAPTER 3

Some missionaries visit churches in search of Muslim- or Hindu-background believers they can siphon off into "more strategic" ministries. One's view of the church matters for missions, and that view won't be taught at a missionary finishing school. It's imbibed, years earlier, through a healthy church culture.

As Andy Johnson, a pastor in Central Asia, says, "Churches are where faithful missionaries are made."[22] No application process can substitute for a missionary's proven involvement in the life of a local church. That's why it's so vital for them to be healthy members—before they go.

### After They Go

The apostle John set the standard for sending churches: "You will do well to send them on their journey *in a manner worthy of God*" (3 John 6). What a high standard! The stakes are high because missionaries "have gone out for the sake of the name" (3 John 7)—not for their own ambition or profit, but to spread the fame, glory, and honor of Jesus Christ. No other priority comes close.

The name of Christ is at stake in churches' ongoing care for their missionaries. Tom Steller, a noted missions mobilizer,

22 Johnson, *Missions*, 46.

says, "God is not glorified when our missionaries are simply a name on the back of the church bulletin or a line item in the budget."[23] The missions cause isn't only for those who go; it's also for those who send. John urged generous support in order that "we may be fellow workers for the truth" (3 John 8). Faithful support of true gospel ministers makes the church an active partner in the greatest cause.

### *Generous Support*

Generally speaking, churches should support missionaries generously and abundantly. As Paul urged Titus, "Do your best to speed Zenas the lawyer and Apollos on their way; see that they lack nothing" (Titus 3:13). One way to meet this standard is to give a high level of support to a few missionaries. Concentrate bigger support toward missionaries whom you implicitly trust and respect. A long list of missionaries in many places around the world is no cause for celebration if they're all given meager support. By focusing support on fewer missionaries, churches can know the details of their workers' ministries and pray more specifically for their needs.

One missionary in the Middle East left his sending organization due to differences in philosophy. This required him to

---

23  Tom Steller, "The Supremacy of God in Going and Sending," afterword in John Piper, *Let the Nations Be Glad* (Grand Rapids, MI: Baker, 1993), 227.

CHAPTER 3

get a job with an engineering firm in order to remain in the country. The sending-church pastor assured the missionary of their continued support, with or without his "tentmaking" employment. "We actually want to give the gospel to the Arabs! If at any time you are in a tight spot, don't hesitate to wire for money. . . . We really are behind you 100 percent." The missionary remained in the region and used his job to reach out even more. Generous financial support honors the Lord.

### *Committed Prayer*

When Paul and Barnabas returned to Antioch, they reported "all that *God* had done with them and how *he* had opened a door of faith to the Gentiles" (Acts 14:27). Since God sovereignly advances his kingdom, prayer is key to success. As Conrad Mbewe urges, "The work of missions should be at the heart of our church prayer meetings."[24]

Clifton Baptist Church in Kentucky prays diligently for the many missionaries they have sent out. Every year, they contact them for updated prayer requests. At their annual women's retreat, they devote a portion of time to praying for their supported overseas workers and then handwrite notes

24  Mbewe, *God's Design for the Church*, 159.

CHURCH AS THE ORIGIN OF MISSIONS

to encourage women in the field. My wife and I (John) have been receiving these notes for twenty years.

### *Helpful Visits*

Overseas ministry can be discouraging. My family has regularly been refreshed by visits from supporting-church elders passing through the region. They care for us. They ask questions about our marriage, family, and spiritual well-being. They pray for us and remind us why we're here. Like Paul and Barnabas, they see how we are (Acts 15:36). Their encouragement fortifies us, and we know the saints back home are praying for us.

Mt. Vernon Baptist Church in Atlanta has a thoughtful approach to overseas visits. Far from being "missionary tourists," visits from this church are generally exploratory (evaluating long-term partnerships); encouraging (blessing workers on the field); equipping (providing training and resources to support strategic work); and evangelistic (engaging in cross-cultural, personal evangelism).[25]

Missions-centered churches not only send and support. Where possible, they directly encourage the work through their presence and ministry resources.

25  Mt. Vernon Baptist Church *Sending* booklet (2023).

CHAPTER 3

*Warm Hospitality*

When missionaries return on furlough, they need practical support—housing, meals, friendship, and counseling. One generous couple at a supporting church loaned us their Audi SUV year after year and drove their pickup truck instead!

Housing missionaries helps not only them—it helps the supporting church. Good things happen when missionaries come home. I remember spending time with one particular missionary who was home on furlough. He had served in Uzbekistan for ten years. As I learned about the challenges and opportunities of his ministry, I was burdened to pray specifically and regularly for a Muslim family who lived across the street from him. Years later, I learned that the family had been converted. This missionary cast a compelling vision for missions and planted seeds in my life that would spring up years later.

## When Should a Church Pull Its Support?

Missions committees, elders, and other decision makers within churches are responsible to support only those missionaries who have "gone out for the sake of the name" (3 John 7). Churches have to know their supported workers—their doctrine, lives, missions philosophy, and on-the-ground ministry practice. This requires discernment, because missionaries

## CHURCH AS THE ORIGIN OF MISSIONS

tend to be respected and implicitly trusted. Elliot Clark observes, "If the false apostles in Corinth were interviewed by the average missions committee, they would no doubt identify themselves as servants of Christ."[26] Even well-intentioned missionaries can be influenced by the prevailing trends of pragmatism, rapid multiplication, and theological minimalism.

Some missionaries are false brothers (2 Cor. 11:26; 1 John 4:1) and should be defunded immediately. Others are simply incompetent and should be removed gradually over time. Not everyone who asks for support is worthy of it (2 John 10).

As our church in Dubai united around a word-oriented ministry philosophy, we realized that some of our supported missionaries weren't on the same page. Some were faithful laborers but operating from a different "ministry grid." Others were living in the United States and had little role in cross-cultural missions. One was morally disqualified. Over time, we reformed our missions budget to reflect our missions strategy. Now we financially partner with stronger, like-minded gospel work that's happening throughout our region. It took years to reform our missions support list and strategy. But churches are responsible for those they send and support.

26  Clark, *Mission Affirmed*, 169.

## CHAPTER 3

### "We Felt Like We Had Never Left"

Leon Blosser was the consummate missionary. In 1964 he began evangelistic work among Bedouin desert tribes in the Trucial States (now known as the UAE). Blosser recalled the flight with his family from Baghdad to the city of Sharjah. Gulf Arabs from the ruling families boarded the plane, "each one with a falcon on his wrist, with a leather sleeve."[27]

Attached to the newly established Oasis Mission Hospital, Blosser knew five of the seven sheikhs (rulers) of the Emirates. His Arabic was so fluent that he was often mistaken for a Palestinian. He wrote the orientation training manual for new missionaries coming onto the field. Between 1969 and 1971 an Arab church came into existence in the oasis town of Al Ain.

Standing behind Blosser was Grace Baptist Church in Carlisle, Pennsylvania. Blosser had come to faith as a teenager and became a charter member of Grace Baptist Church. In that nurturing atmosphere, he developed a growing desire to "be a minister among those who had no knowledge of the gospel."[28] Blosser was a good friend of Grace Baptist's pastor, Walt Chantry. Blosser recalled that Chantry was "a

27 Leon Blosser in an unpublished video.
28 James Eshleman, *Reflections on Grace: A History of Grace Baptist Church* (self-published, 2007), 30.

## CHURCH AS THE ORIGIN OF MISSIONS

tremendous encouragement in regular, warm-hearted correspondence. He took a real interest in what was going on in our lives on the field."

Four years after going to Arabia, when there was sickness in Blosser's family, the pastor wrote, "Believe me, the tempo of our prayers has increased for your health and for God's grace to fill you, and for God's blessings upon the beloved Arabs. Our hearts are also with you. Take care, and preach on. In the love of Christ, Walt" (Feb. 15, 1968).[29] The next year, after updating Blosser on the church back home, Chantry said, "At times like this I wish you were still around the corner so we could bang heads for an hour or so. I deeply miss your fellowship. But our loss is the Arab's gain. Since you have taught us to love them, we will not complain" (Oct. 21, 1969).

Before the days of Zoom, WhatsApp, or email, Pastor Chantry remained current with on-the-ground ministry details: "We pray almost daily for George and Mahmoud [co-laborers in the gospel]. Express our warmest Christian love to them. We have also been praying earnestly that God would save the man you are teaching to read." Chantry was also praying for "the king of Sharjah, the fishermen, etc" (Jan. 19, 1970; March 8, 1974).

29 The following excerpts are from unpublished letters written by Walt Chantry to Leon Blosser.

III

## CHAPTER 3

In 1970, Blosser was sick for weeks on end. Pastor Chantry wrote to him, "Your mother told us that you probably had mononucleosis. You're going to have to stop kissing camels. We really are sorry that you are down again with sickness. We are praying for God to grant you and your family strong health" (Feb. 23, 1970). Concluding another encouraging letter, Chantry wrote, "I wish Dubai were in driving distance so we could have occasional fellowship. But then we have eternity for that, after the labors are done" (Jan. 13, 1972).

Not only the pastor but the whole church was dedicated to prayer. More than eight years after Blosser had been on the field, one of the deacons sent him an updated membership directory and said he was still praying. "Keep circling the walls—it may soon be the seventh time around on the seventh day, and the walls of resistance may soon begin falling down flat. May the Lord hasten the day of visiting in power and great glory" (Feb. 8, 1973). Those are the kinds of prayers a missionary needs. At Christmas in 1975, the church bought Blosser a set of old Samuel Zwemer books on missions. In an accompanying letter, one deacon assured him, "We remember you daily in prayer in our family devotions."

After a supported missionary has been on the field for years, churches can be tempted to lose interest. They can become distracted at home, complacent in prayer, or neglectful in

CHURCH AS THE ORIGIN OF MISSIONS

support. But Grace Baptist was a model sending-church. For decades, it maintained generous support and showed generous hospitality. They sponsored annual missions conferences and translation projects, housed missionaries, and sent out other missionaries to Colombia, New Guinea, Nigeria, and Puerto Rico. In such an environment, it's hardly surprising that Chantry wrote, "I have never seen so many men honestly and prayerfully offering themselves to God for the work of foreign missions" (Dec. 24, 1974).

Blosser was a founding member of the Evangelical Christian Church of Dubai. He led studies in 1 Timothy with fellow church leaders as they considered what it meant to be a biblical church. But his ties were never severed with his church back home. Those ties supported him for decades of ministry in the Arab world.

Throughout the difficulties and trials of a missionary career, Blosser knew his sending church was earnestly praying. "We felt like we were part of a family. We didn't feel like we were 'out there.' We felt like we had never left."

Blosser had been sent by a church. During the 1960s and 70s, he was instrumental in planting congregations (both Arabic and English) on the field. Whether it's Grace Baptist in Carlisle or Kabwata Baptist in Lusaka or the apostle Paul's church in Antioch—the origin of missions is the local church.

# 4

# Church as the
# Means of Missions

There was a time when to be an Armenian was to be Ortho-dox.[1] In 1846, there were no Armenian evangelicals in Istan-bul. But in a small corner of the city William Goodell and other missionaries began teaching the Bible and proclaiming the gospel to Armenian men and women.

Then something happened: A few Armenian Orthodox priests repented and believed the gospel, and then dozens fol-lowed suit. Everyone was full of joy! At first, in an early spirit

---

1 That is, the Eastern church that broke away from the West in the Great Schism of 1054. "Like Rome, the East has a strong sacramental theology: it affirms baptismal regeneration and communion for infants, but it rejects Rome's view of transubstantiation." Steve Wellum, *Systematic Theology: From Canon to Concept* (Brentwood, TN: B&H Academic, 2024), 37.

## CHAPTER 4

of ecumenism, the missionaries opposed starting churches for the new Christians. Instead, they wanted the new disciples to remain within the Orthodox Church to work and pray for its eventual reform.

But reality wiped the idealism away. At the beginning of 1846, the patriarch and leaders of the Armenian Church officially declared the missionaries and their teachings to be "enemies to the holy faith of Christianity."[2] They excommunicated and denounced the new Armenian evangelicals—that is, anyone who embraced the gospel taught by the missionaries. Though he had no official authority to put anyone to death, the patriarch called on former friends and family members of the Armenian evangelicals to commit a kind of "social martyrdom."

Water- and bread-bearers refused to deliver to them, so they began to starve. Some were killed. Though persecuted, they maintained their joy and approached the missionaries who had taught them the Scriptures. Without a church, they were sheep without a shepherd. They longed to worship God in sincere fellowship with other believers.

Cut off from their past Orthodox family, these new Christians acutely felt their need for community. They begged the

2   E. D. G. Prime, *Forty Years in the Turkish Empire* (New York, NY: Robert Carter and Brothers, 1876), 308.

## CHURCH AS THE MEANS OF MISSIONS

missionaries to establish a church! These persecuted Christians led their missionaries.

Thankfully, the missionaries agreed to separate from the Orthodox Church and establish a new work. Goodell wrote,

> I did not expect to live to see this day, but I have seen it and am glad. This has been a most marvellous work of God, and so evident is this, that the nations around say one to another, "The Lord hath done great things for them." Even the [Muslims] have said, "This is the miracle of 1846." I often walk the room, and lift up my hands and say to myself, "Wonderful! Wonderful!"[3]

During a four-and-a-half-hour meeting, forty members constituted the church and about forty more were added as soon as they could be examined. These Armenian believers intuitively understood that the church was central to the Christian life.

In contrast, modern approaches to missions often downplay the church and are forced to rely on human ingenuity.

I (Scott) have attended countless trainings whose message more or less amounts to "This is what you ought to do." During seminary, we studied new methods of missions among

---

3 Prime, *Forty Years*, 317.

## CHAPTER 4

Muslims, including Insider Movements and methods of evangelism that used the Qur'an as a bridge to the Bible. We were told these methods showed promise in being effective at winning Muslims for Christ. Even after moving overseas, we were introduced to a steady stream of new methods that promised results: Church Planting Movements, shadow pastoring, T4T ("Training for Trainers"), "house church only" methods, the Person of Peace method, Universal Disciple, Disciple Making Movements, Four Fields, and Any-3, to name just a few. As the Preacher said, "Of making many books there is no end" (Eccles. 12:12). I have learned a lot from the brothers and sisters who brought us these trainings. I have no doubt their desire was to by all means save some (1 Cor. 9:22). But we must always ensure our desires and methods are governed by Scripture.

What should we make of these different methods? One difficulty of church planting is its inherent ambiguity. For example, imagine you find yourself in the middle of your third year on the mission field and you've witnessed no new converts. You simply aren't sure what you should spend your next day doing. Or imagine you were gathering with five believers but three of them just walked away from the faith. You think, "Now what?" This ambiguity leads many missionaries to give up. It leads others to hunt for a step-by-step "method" or "model" that will provide "success."

## CHURCH AS THE MEANS OF MISSIONS

What happens when church planters on the field have weak ecclesiology? They create methods and models according to their own wisdom.

In this book series, we want to restore the church to the missions conversation. Missions methodology—and, therefore, the day-to-day activity of missionaries—should be centered on the local church. Not only is the local church the origin of missions (see chap. 3) and the end of missions (see chap. 5), but the local church is also the means of missions. That is, missionaries should focus their activity in their local church.

## Holding Your Breath on the Mission Field

When our daughters decided to attend college, my wife and I prioritized helping them find a good church. Thankfully, they both moved to college towns where there were several good congregations. If the situation had been otherwise, that university wouldn't have been an option. We couldn't fathom sending our precious children to a prestigious school if it meant they had to hold their spiritual breath. Christians need healthy churches.

Yet missionaries do the equivalent of this all the time. I once heard of a young man—I'll call him Alex—who served as a missionary in an Arabic-speaking country. Arabic is one of the hardest languages for native English speakers to learn. Alex's field supervisor strongly urged him to join an

CHAPTER 4

Arabic-speaking church because it would help him learn more quickly. Alex didn't feel he had much choice in the matter. So he attended church without understanding much of what was taught. Over time, Alex began to starve. He lacked spiritual care. Finally, after two years, Alex was able to understand the sermon. When he left the worship service, he wept.

Alex had been holding his breath. For two years. While his story turned out okay, it tends to be the exception.

## Should Missionaries Join a Church Overseas?

Previous generations had a higher view of the local church on the field as key to a missionary's well-being and longevity.[4] Henry Martyn, the pioneer missionary to India and Persia, warned of "how great are the temptations of a missionary to neglect his own soul. Apparently outwardly employed for God, my heart has been growing more hard and proud."[5]

This is why, ordinarily, a missionary should join a church on the field. A sentimental attachment to the church "back home" isn't enough. Membership is a mutual promise, a covenant, between a local church and a Christian. The New Testament's

---

4  This section is modified from John Folmar, "Should Missionaries Join a Local Church," Desiring God website, March 28, 2023, https://www.desiringgod.org/.

5  John Sargent, *The Life and Letters of Henry Martyn* (Edinburgh, UK: Banner of Truth, 1985), 214.

120

## CHURCH AS THE MEANS OF MISSIONS

"one another" commands require physical proximity. How can Christians "obey your leaders and submit to them" (Heb. 13:17) or "not neglect to meet together" (10:25) or "let brotherly love continue" (13:1) if they're not in the same church?

The local church is the final earthly court of appeal in matters of discipline and doctrine. It has the exclusive responsibility to affirm or deny the validity of one's profession of faith. Such binding and loosing (Matt. 18:18) makes sense only in the context of a relationship. One cannot be in meaningful membership covenant with someone on another continent.

None of this means missionaries should sever their relationships with their home church when they go overseas. Those relationships endure, but they change. Paul and Barnabas were released by the church at Antioch (Acts 13:3), but they returned and reestablished ministry relationships (Acts 14:27; 15:35; 18:22). Sending churches (and missions agencies) have important roles, but biblical membership and accountability require proximity.

Sending churches can remain committed to and supportive of the missionary's ministry without calling him or her a "member." Clearly, this arrangement is delicate; many overlapping relationships are involved. But this shouldn't surprise us. Missions can't be carried out independently. The work must be cooperative and interdependent. As the Southgate Fellowship puts it, "We affirm that a visible church which sends a missionary, and the

## CHAPTER 4

visible church which a missionary plants or ministers in, share a vital and mutually important relationship."[6]

Not all kinds of authority are the same. To generalize, the division of responsibility looks like this:

- Sending churches affirm, send, and hold the missionary accountable in the task. They exercise *managerial authority*.
- Local churches on the field affirm and hold accountable the missionary in his walk and faith. They exercise *pastoral authority* and *ecclesial authority*, meaning, the binding-and-loosing authority that Jesus gives churches to covenant together as churches and to discipline one another as occasion requires.
- If missions agencies are involved, they typically work alongside the sending church. By equipping and holding the missionary accountable in the task, they also possess *managerial authority*.

One pastor in Central Asia summed it up like this: "A sending church sends, a local church shepherds, a sending organization supervises. To put it negatively, a sending church can stop

6 The Southgate Fellowship, "Affirmations and Denials Concerning World Mission," *Themelios* 45, no. 1 (April 2020): 126. Available at https://thesouthgatefellowship.org/.

## CHURCH AS THE MEANS OF MISSIONS

supporting (decommission) a missionary, a local church can discipline him, a sending organization can fire him."[7]

For their own spiritual growth, and for the health and happiness of their marriages and families, missionaries need the ordinary means of grace. They need pastoral oversight, accountability and discipline, sound teaching, and the Lord's Supper. The Lord grants perseverance and staying power in ministry through the local church. Before they're missionaries, missionaries are Christians. And every Christian needs a local church.

### What about When There Is No Church or No Healthy Church?

When we first moved to Asia, there was no healthy church my wife and I could join. The people we served and among whom we lived were not completely unengaged with the gospel—there were Christians and churches proclaiming Christ to them. But none of these Christians lived within two hundred miles of our city. We were on the frontier.

Two very different circumstances can make joining a healthy local church impossible. First, in some locations, there really are no known Christians or churches to join. In other

---

7 Caleb Greggsen, "Who's in Charge? Authorities in the Life of a Missionary," unpublished paper (2024), 8.

CHAPTER 4

locations, there may be many churches but none of them are healthy. Both of these situations should be temporary (after all, that's why the missionaries are there) and unsurprising (because the missionaries discovered and planned for this situation in their pre-departure research). By mobilizing other families to deploy with them, missionaries can account for the lack of a healthy church. These families can form the core of a small church upon arrival.

For our family, the small church we formed with a core group of other missionary families was critical to our longevity in a hard location. In the early years we gathered regularly for worship and fellowship in our heart language. Meanwhile, we gave ourselves to intense language learning, shared the gospel as we were able, and made as many new friends as possible. Over time, as the whole group gains proficiency in the local language, a worship gathering can transition to the local language and incorporate new local believers. In other words, this church gathering in the heart language of the missionaries is a temporary solution.

Today, many missionaries like Alex forego church involvement until one exists or they're able to worship meaningfully with an existing national church. In our opinion, there's a better alternative. Missionaries should gather intentionally as a small church until a national church exists.

## CHURCH AS THE MEANS OF MISSIONS

A small church may lack strength in numbers, but it more than makes up for that as its members love each other. That love, as we'll see in the next section, is the key to an ongoing portrayal of the gospel to unbelievers.

## Love in the Church as a Means of Missions

The world is watching.

Jesus said that Christians' love for each other should arrest the attention of the world and attest to the truth of the good news. As we love one another, we teach nonbelievers (John 13:34–35). Unbelievers need to see that Christianity isn't just about beliefs; it's also about establishing people into a new family.[8] When people who are so different from one another come together and love each other, the truth of the gospel comes alive. Churches all over the world are full of different kinds of people—men and women, young and old, rich and poor, higher-class and lower-class. Nevertheless, Sunday after Sunday, they come together because one characteristic alone binds them: They love Jesus. This unity can be convincing proof to unbelievers that what we teach about the Father sending the Son to save the world is true (John 17:21).

8   Robert J. Banks, "Loving Family," in *Paul's Idea of Community: The Early House Churches in Their Cultural Setting*, rev. ed. (Peabody, MA: Hendrickson, 1994).

CHAPTER 4

After Nour, a Muslim from Syria, got saved, she was baptized and joined a church in a Middle Eastern country. Although her husband remained self-consciously Muslim, he began attending church with her in order to be a supportive husband. But after seeing the sacrificial love among the church members as they welcomed him into their homes and loved each other across socioeconomic and class distinctions, his attention was drawn to the message of Christ. In time, he repented and believed in the crucified and risen Lord. As his pastor talked with him about turning points in his own journey of coming to faith in Christ, this new Christian mentioned what he had seen in the corporate witness of the church. As he put it, "I knew this must be the kingdom of God; I had never seen love like this before!"

Our love for each other "fills in the gaps" for those who hear the gospel. Our love confirms that our words are true (Titus 2:10). We should be able to say to our nonbelieving friends, "We've spoken of God's love for you. If you want to see a tangible picture of that love, then look around." Ultimately, unbelievers will judge our teaching based on what they see just as much as what they hear.

One of the most shocking and controversial teachings of Christ is that we should forgive those who wrong us. "If [your brother] sins against you seven times in the day,

## CHURCH AS THE MEANS OF MISSIONS

and turns to you seven times, saying, 'I repent,' you must forgive him" (Luke 17:4). Don't rush by those last words: "You *must* forgive."

Unbelievers take note of how we respond when we offend each other. If they're around us for any length of time, they'll see when we annoy each other. They'll see us offend each other. The key is what comes next. They'll either say, "They're just like us!," or "We've seen nothing like that before!" Francis Schaeffer said visible love in a church "means a very simple thing: It means that when I have failed to love my Christian brother, I go to him and say, 'I'm sorry.' That is first."[9] The world has seen enough of what happens when sinful humans, without God's Spirit, disagree. Disagreements produce murder (Gen. 4:8), coveting (Eccles. 4:8), and strife and quarrels (James 4:1). But when people born of the Spirit disagree, love (1 John 3:14), holiness (1 Thess. 3:12–13), agreement (2 Cor. 13:11), and even unity (1 Pet. 3:8) are now possible outcomes. We should be able to say to our nonbelieving friends, "If you want to see a picture of God's forgiveness, look at how we forgive each other."

Without access to see these incredible God-given relational gifts on display, our national nonbelieving friends will be

---

9  Francis Schaeffer, *The Mark of the Christian*, 2nd ed. (Downers Grove, IL: Intervarsity Press, 2006), 37.

## CHAPTER 4

cut off from a depiction of the gospel's power. When they regularly see our good and bad interactions, the local church is a means of missions.

### Peace in the Church as a Means of Missions

An American missionary in Turkey helped an Iranian member of her church find work as a hairdresser. Together with church members from Iraq and Afghanistan, they met with the non-Christian Turkish owner of the salon. Curious about the group, the salon owner asked about the women's nationalities. When the missionary told her, the salon owner replied, "What are all of you doing together? Aren't you supposed to hate each other?" The missionary found the perfect opening to explain the unity these women had through Jesus Christ.

Through the church, nonbelievers will see that the gospel makes peace between people who have serious reasons to remain separate from each other. Even if nonbelievers don't repent and follow Christ, the picture can be attractive. One Muslim friend saw how we corrected, challenged, and encouraged each other and remarked, "You really do love each other. You have an amazing community." The gospel breaks down barriers between people because, despite their differences, they unite over someone infinitely greater: Christ. This is the point Paul makes in Ephesians 2:15–16: "So making peace, [that he] might reconcile us . . . to God in one body through the cross, thereby killing the hostility."

The members of our churches come from dozens of different nations. We're far less homogenous than our local population. When nonbelievers get to know different individuals from our church personally, they wonder, "What could possibly bring *this* group together?" There's one reason we gladly embrace each other as brothers and sisters: We believe in Jesus.

## The Corporate Life of the Church as a Means of Missions

The cities we live in are predominantly Muslim. Mosques are everywhere. A Muslim man may attend any one of these at any time for his daily prayers or to hear the Friday sermon. In a sense, he belongs to all of them. At the same time, he's not a registered member of any of them.

When someone with a Muslim background considers faith in Christ, they may wonder whether biblical Christianity is the same. It isn't. The life of the Christian is one where mutual submission and accountability occur with others who have (a) received new birth from the Holy Spirit, (b) repented and placed their faith in Christ, and (c) committed to live with each other according to the Bible's teachings. When a nonbeliever sees Christians living together as committed church

## CHAPTER 4

members, she'll understand that the Christian life isn't an individual affair. It's a life of intimate community.

### Service in the Church as a Means of Missions

Christians are called to do good deeds. They care for the poor (Gal. 2:10), they share with the needy (Luke 14:12–14), they strengthen the weak (James 1:27). We don't do these good deeds for attention but because we love Jesus. And yet, caring for the poor is a powerful witness for the gospel. One of my wife's closest friends, a Turkish Muslim, lived next door. She heard the gospel a lot but remained unconvinced. One day, when she saw how we handed out food packets to the poor in our city, she said, "What you all are doing is wonderful." She loved our act of love. We hope it led her to reconsider what we taught about God's love in the gospel. The Bible encourages Christians to care for the poor. Peter, James, and John urged the apostle Paul to "remember the poor." Paul says it was "the very thing I was eager to do" (Gal. 2:10).

Historically, Christians have cared for the poor in ways that accent the gospel we preach. During the devastating epidemics of the second and third centuries, Christian leaders and laymen risked and sometimes gave their lives to nurse the suffering back to health. Some historians believe that Christians' simple nursing techniques significantly cut mortality

## CHURCH AS THE MEANS OF MISSIONS

rates and provided a positive witness for Christianity.[10] The Christians' response stood in such stark contrast to their pagan neighbors who fled the cities that non-Christian Roman rulers like Julian became concerned that many citizens would convert to Christianity.

First John 3:17–18 says, "If anyone has the world's goods and sees his brother in need, yet closes his heart against him, how does God's love abide in him? Little children, let us not love in word or talk but in deed and in truth." Because of verses like these, by the fourth century monks developed a system of healthcare.[11] Basil of Caesarea constructed his famous "Basileiad," which included a school, an orphanage, quarters for the poor, and a hospital.

When churches care for the poor, they gain goodwill, which can be a positive development for the gospel (Acts 2:47). Around the world, Christians are known for their generosity. Several years ago, a public school in a poor neighborhood of Istanbul needed fifteen thousand dollars for an addition to their building. They reached out to a small national church in their neighborhood. One member of that church,

---

10 Rodney Stark, *The Rise of Christianity: A Sociologist Reconsiders History* (Princeton, NJ: Princeton University Press, 1996), 77–90.

11 Robert Louis Wilken, *The First Thousand Years: A Global History of Christianity* (New Haven, CT: Yale University Press, 2013), 159.

CHAPTER 4

Halime, immediately reached out to her broad network of Christian friends around Turkey. Within just a few days, she raised the full amount. Halime asked the donors how they would like the gift delivered, since donors usually want to receive credit for the gift. But these friends were all insistent: The funds would be given only if the gift came from Halime's church. The neighborhood was thrilled, and the reputation of this small church grew.

It's important to care for the poor, but churches should be careful that their work doesn't overwhelm their primary cause. Churches care for the sick, but they shouldn't become hospitals. Churches provide food for the hungry, but they shouldn't become soup kitchens. More than healthcare and hunger prevention, our neighborhoods need the gospel, and only local churches are entrusted with that message.

At the same time, we don't care for the poor simply to convert them. Christians didn't place themselves at risk only when they could be sure of conversions. Our job is faithfulness; God's job is conversion. Christians sacrifice their lives because they're convinced the word of God is true, because they want to provide a positive witness for Christ in the world. Local church members provide a powerful witness for the gospel when they pool their resources and coordinate efforts to care for those in need.

## Discipleship in the Church as a Means of Missions

Churches evangelize unbelievers, but they also help believers to grow. In other words, the church is a means of both evangelism and discipleship.

The ideal community for growth is a church, in which a body of committed believers learn from qualified elders and patiently but persistently grow together. Growth involves more than merely learning Scripture's commands. It involves more than knowing and approving and even communicating those commands to others. Being a disciple means learning how to obey what the Bible teaches us (Matt. 18:20), and this happens best in local churches.

My good friend Mehmet was a bright, good-looking young man who had professed faith in Christ while living in a small village. He moved to attend college in our city. Upon arriving, the first thing he did was connect with our small church. He loved the Bible, and he loved being a Christian. But he'd never lived as a member of a local church. As a result, certain sins had gone unnoticed.

In our country, sexual promiscuity is widespread even as sexual immorality is culturally frowned upon. It's as if people know sexual sin is wrong but they think they can't help themselves. Mehmet brought these cultural assumptions

CHAPTER 4

with him as a new Christian. In the Bible, he saw a sexual ethic that aligned with his cultural background. As we studied the Bible together, we encouraged each other to sexual purity and warned each other of the spiritual dangers of impurity. Eventually, his new community of Christians found out about his loose living. We all tried to help him. We rebuked him individually and committed to pray with him and for him.

I wish I could report that he "got it." He didn't. One more step was needed. Though he hid it well, Mehmet persisted in his sin. We discussed the sad situation with the whole church. It was clear: Mehmet showed no repentance. So the church voted unanimously to place him under discipline.

These actions all helped Mehmet learn how to obey Christ's commands for sexual purity. We confronted his unrepentance. His church community, with one voice, communicated what God expected of him. Thankfully, he repented and was reinstated to fellowship. Once restored, Mehmet grew in the Lord as he served fruitfully in his church. In this way, our whole congregation carried out the Great Commission. We taught him to observe all that Jesus commanded (Matt. 28:20).

This type of discipline—usually called "corrective" or "restorative" discipline—trains disciples to obey Christ. It

## CHURCH AS THE MEANS OF MISSIONS

reverberated throughout our church as Mehmet and other members grew. This incident also helped our evangelism as close unbelieving friends outside our church heard how seriously we took this sin.

But there's another kind of discipline too. Regulative discipline occurs through the church's regular, ongoing activity. Think Bible studies, corporate prayers, café conversations, listening to sermons, and singing psalms, hymns, and spiritual songs—all the ordinary stuff of the Christian life in the church. This kind of discipline changes us day after day and week after week as we continue to gather regularly (Heb. 3:13).

If this is the experience of "normal" Christians, then we should expect it for our missionaries too.

Discipled missionaries will endure. A World Evangelical Alliance study determined that lack of pastoral care contributes to many missionaries returning home earlier than expected.[12] A follow-up study showed pastoral care remains "very poor" among these gospel ministers.[13]

---

12 Rodolfo "Rudy" Girón, "An Integrated Model of Missions," in *Too Valuable to Lose: Exploring the Causes and Cures of Missionary Attrition*, ed. William D. Taylor (Pasadena, CA: William Carey Library, 1997), 38.

13 Ken Caruthers, *The Missionary Team as Church: Applied Ecclesiology in the Life and Relationships between Cross-Cultural Church Planters* (PhD diss., Southeastern Baptist Theological Seminary, 2014), 90.

## CHAPTER 4

It doesn't have to be this way. Christians thrive when they're together; they struggle when they're on their own.[14] We've been privileged to know missionaries from all kinds of sending agencies and backgrounds. Too often, we've encountered the strange situation where missionaries live near good healthy churches yet are unable to join those churches because their sending agency won't let them. These situations shouldn't exist!

When the church is the method of missions, missionaries will have pastoral care, just as the Bible intends for all Christians.

### Sending from the Church as a Means of Missions

A friend of mine moved with his wife and son to live among people in Papua New Guinea who had never heard the gospel. They left their extended family and home church to move across the world. At significant financial cost, they established their new home in a remote village. For ten long years, my friend learned the local language, created a system to write it down, translated the Bible, and taught the local people the Scriptures. Even after men and women in the village professed faith in Christ, he stayed. He didn't want to just turn to the

14 Joseph H. Hellerman, *When the Church Was a Family: Recapturing Jesus's Vision for Authentic Christian Community* (Nashville: B&H, 2009), 1.

## CHURCH AS THE MEANS OF MISSIONS

next village and repeat what he'd done. Instead, he cared for these new, heroic disciples of Jesus. In the face of significant persecution from family members and villagers who rejected the gospel, they were baptized and formed a faithful, healthy church. Years later, these saints are still proclaiming the gospel to nearby villages.

This is God's ancient plan. We see this is Isaiah 66:

The time is coming to gather all nations and tongues. And they shall come and shall see my glory, and I will set a sign among them. And from them I will send survivors to the nations . . . that have not heard my fame or seen my glory. And they shall declare my glory among the nations. (66:18–19)

What a plan! God says, "I will gather them. . . . They will see my glory. . . . They will declare my glory to the nations." God will draw people out of the nations to gaze in wonder at his glory. He will send some of these people back to declare God's glory to the nations who haven't yet believed.

How wonderful that God doesn't need Western missionaries to spread the gospel to every new village! Underreached people won't be evangelized by sending a steady stream of expat missionaries. Instead, they will hear the gospel as mature churches are established. This is Jesus's missions strategy.

CHAPTER 4

## Conclusion

The church is the origin and means of missions. As it remains at the center of missions, it will become a discipleship factory that sends a steady stream of new disciples to the nations.

We've come full circle: Churches that were started through missionary efforts become the origin for sending and starting more churches. Through these yet-to-be-started churches, the gospel is not only established *among* these nations but *from* these nations—all for the glory of God.

When those first Armenian Christians were converted in July 1846, they immediately understood the necessity of the church in the Christian life. Their new church wasn't just the fruit of missionary activity. It became the means of life for the new disciples and the means of more missions activities in the decades to come. Though this church began in great weakness, it still gathers in Istanbul to this day as a witness to the miracle of 1846.

I walked past the church recently. The placard next to the entrance reads triumphantly: "The First Armenian Evangelical Church of the World."

5

# Church as the
# Goal of Missions

The UAE is known for its glitz and glamour. Shopping malls dot the landscape. Skyscrapers rise from the desert. Beneath the ground are 113 billion barrels of crude oil reserves.[1] Foreigners flock here to build careers and amass wealth.

But it wasn't always this way.

Late one night in September 1968, three years before the UAE became a nation, a Bedouin woman was giving birth at the Oasis Hospital, a Christian mission hospital a hundred miles into the Arabian desert. Complications required a C-section, and the mother needed blood. A member of the missions staff who was there recalled personnel "chasing

---

1  "UAE Facts and Figures," OPEC website, 2024, https://www.opec.org/.

## CHAPTER 5

around to all the companies at midnight trying to find a donor with the right blood type."[2] Out of fifty people tested, only the attending physician, Dr. Marian Kennedy, and one of the nurses had the right blood type. The doctor interrupted the procedure, gave blood herself, and then completed the delivery.

The good work Dr. Kennedy did that night actually began a decade earlier. In 1959, her husband, Dr. Burwell Kennedy, had taken a survey trip to the area. Here's what he wrote: "A hospital there would be easily accessible to the Bedu of the desert, to the mountain tribes in their isolated villages, and to the many travelers, hunters, and other visitors passing to and fro."[3] Prior to the mission hospital's work, infant and maternal mortality rates stood at 50 percent and 35 percent, respectively. So the married doctors started a hospital. After 1960, those mortality rates plummeted, and more and more Gulf Arabs went to the Oasis for childbirth. The current president of the UAE, Sheikh Mohammed bin Zayed Al Nahyan, was born there in 1961. The groundwork was laid for mutual respect and good relations between evangelical Christians and the Emirati people; it predated the nation

2 Correspondence from J. Melhuish to Leon Blosser, Sept. 19, 1968.
3 "Arabian Gulf Handbook of the Evangelical Alliance Mission (TEAM)" (un-published, 1965), 14.

itself. The local people have often said of evangelicals: "You loved us *before* the oil."

Though the hospital alleviated much suffering in the region, this wasn't the Kennedys' ultimate goal. One of the early hospital missionaries said, "Our personal goal was to see an Arab congregation that would grow up there and flourish and share the gospel." The hospital was a means to an end— churches among the Arabian desert tribes.

Missions requires not just good deeds but gospel proclamation. The aim of gospel proclamation isn't individual converts but churches that display the glory of God. As Conrad Mbewe says,

> We may need to establish hospitals and schools. We may need to supply food, clothing and shelter. There is nothing wrong with that as long as we do not begin to see these as an end in themselves. Our primary work in missions is evangelism and the planting of churches after the New Testament pattern—churches that will continue this same work long after we are gone.[4]

Church planting is how the Great Commission will be fulfilled.

4   Conrad Mbewe, *Foundations for the Flock* (Hannibal, MO: Granted Ministries Press, 2011), 299.

CHAPTER 5

## Evangelism ≠ Missions

We heartily embrace John Piper's dictum "Missions exists because worship doesn't."[5] Missions is ultimately for the glory of God. So why do we say that the end-goal of missions is the *church*? It's because the church on earth is where the "manifold wisdom of God" shines forth (Eph. 3:10). The world has been plunged into the darkness of spiritual alienation (5:8), but Jesus told his disciples, "You are the light of the world" (Matt. 5:14). Assemblies of ordinary, unsophisticated people are the means by which the world will be enlightened! This is why the book of Revelation refers to the seven churches in Asia Minor as "lampstands" whose purpose is to radiate the light of God's glory in the gospel of Jesus Christ (Rev. 2:1).

Evangelism is vital to missions but it's not synonymous with missions. Think of it this way: A fruitful evangelistic conversation is like lighting one candle. You strike a match, and a candle is lit—praise God! But one candle lights only a small space. And it can be easily blown out. Think of the church as a bonfire, a blazing witness to God's perfect character that multiplies gospel influence in the area. It may take longer to start a bonfire, but the light will still be shining long after you leave.

---

5  John Piper, *Let the Nations Be Glad!*, vol. 3, *The Collected Works of John Piper* (Wheaton, IL: Crossway, 2017), 447.

CHURCH AS THE GOAL OF MISSIONS

The Great Commission will be fulfilled not simply by more individuals being converted but by new congregations being formed. This doesn't involve less than evangelism and conversion, but it does involve more. Missions necessarily involves the verbal proclamation of the gospel, but it also includes teaching everything Jesus commanded, which takes a church.

When Paul and Barnabas proclaimed Christ in Asia Minor, Luke tells us they "made many disciples" (Acts 14:21). But they also planted churches. How do we know? A few verses later, we learn they returned to the same places where disciples had been made and "appointed elders for them in every church" (14:23). In other words, they left churches behind, even though they didn't yet have elders. But they knew those churches needed elders so they returned quickly and appointed them. Paul did something similar in Crete. He instructed Titus to remain in Crete to "put what remained into order, and appoint elders in every town" (Titus 1:5). Until an indigenous biblical church was formed, complete with elder-qualified local leadership, Paul and Barnabas knew their task wasn't done.

## Not Bricks but Buildings

When the apostle Paul wrote his letter to the Romans, he had "fulfilled the ministry of the gospel of Christ" throughout a

CHAPTER 5

thousand-mile swath of territory from Jerusalem to Illyrica (Rom. 15:19). It had taken Paul about twenty years, but now he was finished there. Obviously, not every person in every village had heard the good news and believed. So how could Paul say he was finished? He considered his task complete because churches were planted throughout the region.[6] So he passed the torch on to them.

Jesus Christ commissioned Paul to open the eyes of the Gentiles, so that "they may receive forgiveness of sins *and a place among those who are sanctified by faith in me*" (Acts 26:18). The gospel (forgiveness of sins) and membership in the church (a place among the sanctified) always go together. This accords with the earliest days of the church. At Pentecost, "those who received his [Peter's] word were baptized, and there were added that day about three thousand souls" (2:41). Conrad Mbewe explains, "They did not just hold crusades and count the heads of those coming forward after the sermon. . . . They initiated these individuals into local churches."[7] This is why Phil Newton argues, "The goal of mission was the formation of a new community in Christ. . . . Churches, as 'beachhead of the

6  Thomas Schreiner, *Romans*, 2nd ed. (Grand Rapids, MI: Baker Academic, 2018), 744.

7  Mbewe, *Foundations*, 299.

## CHURCH AS THE GOAL OF MISSIONS

new creation,' inevitably resulted by obedience to Christ's Commission."[8]

Small phrases sprinkled throughout Paul's letters show that the apostle thought corporately about ministry:

- "All the churches of Christ greet you" (Rom. 16:16).
- "I teach them everywhere in every church" (1 Cor. 4:17).
- "We ourselves boast about you in the churches of God" (2 Thess. 1:4).

The Bible is a missions manual. J. H. Bavinck observed, "The epistles and the book of Revelation were written on the mission field."[9] And yet all of Paul's letters were written to churches or were intended to be read by them. Paul Bowers said, "Paul pictures himself not as a maker of bricks but as a builder of buildings."[10] He was founding communities, not only converting individuals.

---

8  Phil Newton, *The Mentoring Church: How Pastors and Congregations Cultivate Leaders* (Grand Rapids, MI: Kregel, 2017), 43, 46, quoting Johannes Nissen, *New Testament and Mission: Historical and Hermeneutical Perspectives*, 3rd ed. (Frankfurt am Main: Peter Lang, 2004), 111.

9  J. H. Bavinck, *An Introduction to the Science of Missions* (Phillipsburg, NJ: P&R, 1960), 42.

10  Paul Bowers, "Fulfilling the Gospel: The Scope of the Pauline Mission," in *The Journal of the Evangelical Theological Society* 30 (1987): 188.

CHAPTER 5

Paul wasn't in a frantic hurry to evangelize the nations. He wasn't anxious to be freed from nurturing churches in order to press forward toward the frontier. For eighteen months, he remained in Corinth, "teaching the word of God among them" (Acts 18:11). In Ephesus, when Paul was run out of the synagogue, he "took the disciples with him, reasoning daily in the hall of Tyrannus. This continued for two years, so that all the residents of Asia heard the word of the Lord, both Jews and Greeks" (19:9–10).

Paul regularly slowed down. His goal was "that we may present everyone mature in Christ" (Col. 1:28). He didn't check a box once a city was "reached." His aim was strengthening the churches he had established.

### "Sideways Energy"

Agencies that celebrate movement-driven missions are out of step with apostolic practice, and they bear bitter fruit over the long term.

Michael moved to a cosmopolitan city in Vietnam to reach and equip the local people with the gospel. He immediately began attending a small English-language fellowship. After only two weeks, he was asked to preach. When he asked church leaders if they wanted to know about his beliefs, they declined. "This is an open and inclusive space," they said.

## CHURCH AS THE GOAL OF MISSIONS

Unsurprisingly, this church was weak and ineffective. It wasn't a place Michael could bring new Christians and curious non-Christians. When Vietnamese nationals began coming to faith, he recalled, "There was no place to take them." Every option for church seemed bad. The registered Vietnamese churches preached moralism, and the house churches preached the prosperity gospel. When one local woman believed the gospel and began attending a traditional church, the leaders condemned her because of her tattoos. When another local believer had to stop attending church for a season because she was on bed rest the last months of a pregnancy, the deacons warned her, "God will let your baby die if you don't return." When more locals came to faith, Michael wondered what to do.

He decided to form a new church that would focus on sound doctrine and biblical preaching. He hoped such a church would be a model for missionaries and new converts. But Michael's agency leaders didn't approve. "You're supposed to be doing mobilization," they said. For them, Michael's church was dismissed as "sideways energy." They belittled it as "that *thing* Michael is doing." Nevertheless, he pressed forward, and an unregistered underground house church formed. It had three elders—two Western, one Vietnamese. And it had a clear statement of faith and a church covenant. Michael said, "A beachhead had been established."

There's now a faithful church in this city of more than 1.5 million people. Twenty more like-minded American missionaries joined the work over a two-year period. Workers stay longer. They rub shoulders with Vietnamese nationals and team up for ministry. They learn the language. This church is here to stay. And when indigenous churches led by local leaders are planted, faithful English-language churches like this one can still serve as models and bridges to more ministry.

## D-Minus Church

*Perspectives on the World Christian Movement*, a book edited by Ralph Winter and Steven Hawthorne, accompanies a missions mobilization course called Perspectives. This resource has influenced a generation of missionaries, pastors, and missions committees. It includes some helpful articles but also several bad ones, especially related to the subject of church planting.

In modern missions, ministry dedicated to the ordinary means of grace is sometimes criticized as a "slow to grow" approach. Donald McGavran, one of the early spokesmen for movement-driven missions, once asked, "Whom do they get? They get a man here, a woman there, a boy here, a girl

## CHURCH AS THE GOAL OF MISSIONS

there. . . . That is a sure way to guarantee that any churches started will be small, non-growing, one-by-one churches."[11]

McGavran's alternative was called "People Movements," where entire villages or clans are baptized together. "The principle is to try to get group decisions for Christ."[12] Teaching is downplayed; reproducibility is highlighted. One of McGavran's disciples admitted, "This definition of a church might get a D minus where you studied theology, but the more you add to it, the harder it will be for the churches you start to reproduce."[13] The assumption is clear: Their technique yields evangelistic results, and other approaches are dismissed as "a slow way."[14]

A Western missionary to India was dismayed when his agency shifted strategies. Suddenly, it began urging rapid growth by planting a new church every three to four months. The agency was swayed by movement-driven missions. Here's how one

---

11  Donald McGavran, "A Church in Every People: Plain Talk About a Difficult Subject," in *Perspectives on the World Christian Movement*, ed. Ralph Winter and Stephen Hawthorne, 4th ed. (Pasadena, CA: William Carey Library, 2009), 628. McGavran criticized traditional missions practice where "all seekers are carefully screened to make sure they really intend to receive Christ," 627. Such individual screening, according to McGavran, is too slow.

12  McGavran, "A Church in Every People," 630.

13  George Patterson, "The Spontaneous Multiplication of Churches," in *Perspectives on the World Christian Movement*, ed. Ralph Winter and Stephen Hawthorne, 4th ed. (Pasadena, CA: William Carey Library, 2009), 639.

14  McGavran, "Church in Every People," 632.

## CHAPTER 5

proponent explained his church planting success: "Church Planting Movements [CPMs] reproduce like rabbits!"[15] He then proceeded to note that the gestation period for elephants is twenty-two months, but it's only three months for rabbits. "Elephant churches" are large, inflexible, and slow. Rabbit churches, on the other hand, are nimble, adaptable, and contextualized. In a CPM, new churches are expected to reproduce like rabbits.

But at what cost? These churches sacrifice sound doctrine, trained leaders, and mature discipleship. They are susceptible to false teaching, heresy, and syncretism. Urged to adopt new tactics, the missionary in India candidly replied, "But rabbit churches get eaten by hawks and wolves."[16]

## Straw Man Arguments

Proponents of movement-driven missions sometimes paint opposing viewpoints with an unhelpfully broad brush. "Straw man arguments" present binary alternatives that cloud complicated issues. In *Contagious Disciple Making*, David and Paul Watson criticize "Branded Christianity" as ineffective and slow. The authors conclude, "Organizations that promote a

---

15 David Garrison, *Church Planting Movements: How God Is Redeeming a Lost World* (Midlothian, VA: WIGtake Resources, 2004), 194.

16 Aubrey Suqueira, "A Plea for Gospel Sanity" in *9Marks Journal* (Fall, 2015), 7. Predictably, mass reversions back to Hinduism have occurred.

particular brand of Christianity will have difficulty completing the Great Commission."[17]

They make their case with straw man arguments:

1. "When institutions that promote a particular brand of Christianity forget their differences and get back to planting the Gospel instead of their doctrines, we may have a chance to complete the Great Commission."[18]

*Our reply:* The gospel is "the word of truth" (Eph. 1:13), a message that demands to be accurately proclaimed. Paul urged Titus to "teach what accords with sound doctrine" (Titus 2:1). No wise teacher would drive a wedge between *the gospel* and *doctrine*.

2. In branded Christianity "leaders must go through extensive educational and indoctrination processes before they are allowed to lead."[19] This slows down missions efforts.

*Our reply:* Leading a church is serious business. As James warned, "Not many of you should become teachers, my

---

17  David Watson and Paul Watson, *Contagious Disciple-Making* (Nashville: Thomas Nelson, 2014), 23.

18  Watson and Watson, *Contagious Disciple-Making*, 26.

19  Watson and Watson, *Contagious Disciple-Making*, 25. Recent movement missiologists reiterate this point. For example, Warrick Farah and Alan Hirsh complain that traditional church-planting efforts are hampered, in part, because "Professionals do the ministry." Farah and Hirsch, "Movemental Ecclesiology: Recalibrating Church for the Next Frontier," Academia website, 2021, https://www.academia.edu/.

CHAPTER 5

brothers, for you know that we who teach will be judged with greater strictness" (James 3:1). Paul exhorted Timothy to study hard to be an unashamed workman who "rightly [handles] the word of truth" (2 Tim. 2:15). Church leaders must be "able to teach" (1 Tim. 3:2) and to rebuke those who contradict sound doctrine (Titus 1:9). None of this requires formal seminary training, though such training can be helpful. To label such expectations "indoctrination" is unfortunate and short-sighted.

3. If only institutions that promote branded Christianity would "forget their pet doctrines and practices, we [would] see the Great Commission fulfilled in a generation."[20]

*Our reply:* Jesus instructed us to make disciples and to "teach all that [he] commanded" (Matt. 28:20). We can distinguish Scripture's "primary doctrines," which are necessary for salvation, from its "secondary doctrines," which are not. And yet, the secondary doctrines that pertain to organizing a church—ordinances, leadership, and so on—are necessary for obedience, for the church's witness, and for preserving the gospel from one generation to the next.

That's what a healthy church does. It displays and protects the gospel over time. The apostles didn't practice doctrinal

20  Watson and Watson, *Contagious Disciple-Making*, 27.

## CHURCH AS THE GOAL OF MISSIONS

minimalism, and the Holy Spirit doesn't mean for us to pick and choose which commands to obey. Downplaying scriptural truth goes against the Great Commission. Further, how can anyone know if the Great Commission will be fulfilled within a generation? Jesus himself said, "It is not for you to know times or seasons that the Father has fixed by his own authority" (Acts 1:7).

4. "Our mission is to find and develop Christ followers rather than church members."[21]

*Our reply:* What's the difference between these two? Why build on false dichotomies? In the New Testament, Christ followers are church members, and church members are Christ followers. Sure, church membership will look a little different from context to context. But we shouldn't confuse the biblical element with different cultural forms.

5. "Simply gathering a group of people who subscribe to a common set of beliefs is not worthy of Jesus and the sacrifice he made for us."[22]

*Our reply:* Paul wanted churches to adhere to a "standard of teaching" (Rom. 6:17; see also 1 Cor. 15:3; 2 Tim. 1:13,

---

21 Neil Cole, "Organic Church," in *Perspectives on the World Christian Movement*, 4th ed., ed. Ralph Winter and Stephen Hawthorne (Pasadena, CA: William Carey Library, 2009), 645.

22 Cole, "Organic Church," 645.

CHAPTER 5

Jude 3). Nine times he tells Timothy and Titus to give themselves to sound doctrine, sound teaching, and sound words. He tells the Galatians to remove any teacher who didn't come with the gospel he had taught them (Gal. 1:6–9). Do we really want to contradict Paul and say that churches don't need to subscribe to a common set of sound beliefs? Of course, such belief must be genuine and not mere intellectual assent, since "faith apart from works is dead" (James 2:26). But, again, let's dispense with the false dichotomies.

6. "In some Christian ministry, we assess how mature a believer is based on how much he knows. But the New Testament assesses the maturity of a believer based on how much he obeys."[23]

*Our reply:* Another false dichotomy, as is the case with so much bad teaching. True knowledge is the basis for true obedience. It is because Paul "knows whom I have believed" that he is able to "suffer as I do" in costly obedience (2 Tim. 1:12). By emphasizing obedience over against that knowledge, we risk advocating "zeal without knowledge" (see Rom. 10:2).

7. "Teaching heavy theology *before* one learns loving, childlike obedience is dangerous."[24]

23 Steve Smith with Ying Kai, *T4T: A Discipleship Re-Revolution* (Monument, CO: WIGTAKE Resources, 2011), 79.

24 Patterson, "Spontaneous Multiplication of Churches," 639.

CHURCH AS THE GOAL OF MISSIONS

*Our reply:* Again, false dichotomy. Childlike obedience *results* from sound doctrine. If "heavy" theology means boring and irrelevant and misapplied, then we aren't in favor of that. But the basic fundamentals of the gospel are profound and deep. As believers grow spiritually, the "new self . . . is being renewed in knowledge" (Col. 3:10; see Rom. 12:2).

———

Sound missions practices require careful contextualization. Rigid traditionalism doesn't save. We have no interest in promoting a "brand," unless that "brand" is believing Scripture is sufficient to guide our missions practices. In church-centered missions, our first and final authority is God's word rightly applied to any given context.

## Zuckerberg's Zeal

Facebook's founder Mark Zuckerberg wants every human being on earth to be online. As of the writing of this book, the number of Facebook's monthly active users exceeds the population of India and China combined. That's not enough, Zuckerberg says.

For Zuckerberg, universal social connectivity is the greatest cause on earth. He'll pursue every strategy imaginable in order to fulfill this mission. Our cause—making disciples among all nations—far surpasses the promise of social connectivity

CHAPTER 5

and advertising revenue. So what's our strategy? It's church-centered missions.

We feel the same sense of urgency as the proponents of movement-driven missions. We long for conversions and evangelistic breakthroughs all over the world. After all, the gospel is the "power of God for salvation to *everyone* who believes" (Rom. 1:16). We think of David Brainerd, who tried to reach eighteenth-century Native Americans. He said, "I had a strong hope, that God would 'bow the heavens and come down' and do some marvelous work among the Heathen."[25] May the Lord do so in our generation!

During the eighteenth-century's Great Awakening, Jonathan Edwards wrote to friends in England and described the extraordinary outpouring of God's Spirit. He called his work "A Faithful Narrative of the Surprising Work of God in the Conversion of Many Hundred Souls in Northampton." Edwards sent what he wrote to Isaac Watts who had experienced a similar revival on the other side of the Atlantic.

Should we expect continual revivals? Should we adopt techniques designed to spark rapid multiplication?

Here's what Watts wrote about revivals: "[They are] *rare* instances, and bestowed by the Spirit of God in so sovereign

---

25  Iain Murray, *The Puritan Hope* (Edinburgh, UK: Banner of Truth, 1971), xiii.

and arbitrary a manner, according to the secret counsels of his own wisdom, that no particular Christian hath any sure ground to *expect* them."[26] We should pray for revivals. We should hope for them. We should work hard in evangelism. But we should never try to reverse engineer them. Our hope isn't in our technique or a silver-bullet strategy. It's in the Lord who saves.

We wonder if movement-driven missionaries would title Edwards's work differently. We wonder if they wouldn't call it a "surprising" work of God, but a *guaranteed* work of God. If we do it right, it's like clockwork, right? The Watsons contend, "A Disciple Making Movement is causative; a Church Planting Movement [CPM] is the result."[27] Mike Shipman claims his Any-3 method is "a way of sharing that is proving effective in unlocking people's willingness to say yes to Jesus."[28]

If you're a faithful missionary laboring in hard places where you are *not* seeing fruit, then what would you conclude? That you're doing something wrong? The International Mission

---

26 Quoted in Iain Murray, *Revival & Revivalism* (Edinburgh, UK: Banner of Truth, 1994), 385n1. Emphasis added.

27 Watson and Watson, *Contagious Disciple-Making*, 7.

28 Mike Shipman, *Any-3: Anyone, Anywhere, Anytime* (Monument, CO: WIGTake, 2013), 15. See also S. Kebreab's observation that "Christian history demonstrates the only way that peoples are ever reached is through movements." *Motus Dei: The Movement of God to Disciple the Nations*, ed. W. Farah (Littleton, CO: William Carey, 2021), 35.

CHAPTER 5

Board's Zane Pratt says that some movement-driven missions tend to assume that "if there is no CPM, the problem lies with the worker."[29]

Movement-based missionaries affirm the sovereignty of God in missions and the Holy Spirit's indispensable role in revivals. But their obvious reliance on methods reveals an underlying pragmatism. One movement-driven missionary said this about Church Planting Movements: "It sounded so Acts-like that immediately I knew in my spirit that this should be normative for our mission work."[30]

We disagree. The Lord commends those who hold fast to the word and "bear fruit with patience" (Luke 8:15). Modern missions methods emphasize speed, and therefore there's a growing impatience with strategies that rarely yield explosive, immediate results.

Consider how our Lord described kingdom work: "First the blade, then the ear, then the full grain in the ear" (Mark 4:28). Meanwhile, we're called to keep sowing the seed. David Livingstone penetrated the interior of Africa with the gospel in the mid-1800s. He noted in his journal, "A quiet audience

---

29  Zane Pratt, unpublished review of "Training for Trainers," 21. Pratt says, "It is cruel to hard-working, faithful workers who have not seen many people come to Christ to say that it is their fault."

30  Smith, *T4T: A Discipleship Re-Revolution*, 37.

## CHURCH AS THE GOAL OF MISSIONS

today. The seed being sown, the least of all seeds now, but it will grow into a mighty tree."[31] Jesus's commission for worldwide operations calls for urgency, not hurry.

### Churchless in Niger

In the bush of southern Niger, Esther, a young, single missionary, was suffering from malaria. As her condition worsened, she began convulsing and eventually lost consciousness for two days. When her mission team leader was asked to take her to the hospital in the nearest town, he declined. "The locals don't even go to the hospital." Esther had no spouse or child to speak up for her. Eventually, a roommate intervened, and team members got Esther the required medical care.

The terrorist organization Boko Haram had begun operating nearby, only thirty kilometers away. When the same team leader was asked if there was a contingency plan, he had the team read some psalms together and said, "We don't need a contingency plan."

These missionaries had a problem. Reckless leadership, for one. But they also had no church. They'd decided not

---

31 Quoted in Murray, *Puritan Hope*, 182. William Carey encouraged his son along these lines, urging patience in ministry: "The conversion of one soul is worth the labor of a life. . . . Hold on, therefore; be steady in your work, and leave the result with God." In Timothy George, *Faithful Witness: The Life and Mission of William Carey* (Worcester, PA: Christian History Institute, 1998), 114.

CHAPTER 5

to partner with a nearby congregation. And they didn't constitute as a church themselves. There was no elder-qualified leadership, no biblical accountability, and no administration of the Lord's Supper. When agency leadership called for periodic meetings, the missionaries were warned by the team leader, "Be careful what you say. They don't understand our context." Esther recalled, "We were completely rogue." The team assembled for prayer and teaching, but they were alone in the bush of the Sahel, without the body of Christ. "The leaders were adventurers, not elders," she said.

What was the primary problem? Esther concluded, "We weren't aligned on what church is." According to the team leader, a church popped up whenever two or three Christians hung out. Qualified elders, biblical ordinances, church oversight on the field—these were unnecessary impediments to the mission.

Esther nearly lost her life in southern Niger. Thankfully, her team leaders are no longer there. Reflecting on this, she said, "Sustainable long-term missions has to be connected to the church."

## Missiology Needs Ecclesiology

For two years, William Carey kept a detailed journal to update the Baptist Missionary Society on his work. The journal

## CHURCH AS THE GOAL OF MISSIONS

makes for some inspiring reading. But it also shows frontier missions can be mundane. Here's one entry from July 3, 1793: "Nothing remarkable." That's it. Just an ordinary day. Here's another: "All this week nothing of moment occurred" (June 17–22, 1793).[32] Granted, Carey and his family were cooped up on a ship somewhere near latitude 46° north, longitude 5° west. But ask any frontier missionary, and he'll tell you: Missions often means slogging through ordinary workweeks.

But there were some exciting times, like when Carey had to travel with his family through impenetrable forests to get to their new home in India. In these forests, he said, "There are many serpents and tigers." In fact: "They swarm with tigers." During Carey's first year there, twenty men were "carried away" by them![33]

Upon arriving in India, Carey realized that his finances were inadequate. He faced major tensions in his marriage and on his missions team. He lacked the required immigration permits. He didn't know the language. By all accounts, the obstacles were immense. From his journal, it's obvious that Carey felt the pressure. "Nothing but

32 Terry Carter, *Journal and Selected Letters of William Carey* (Macon, GA: Smyth & Helwys, 2000) 4, 5.

33 Carter, *Journal and Selected Letters*, 9, 15, 25.

## CHAPTER 5

care, worldliness, and anxiety today—may it be buried in oblivion" (April 12, 1794).[34] After his first year, Carey summed up his experience: "When I first left England my hope of the conversion of the heathen was very strong, but among so many obstacles it would entirely die away, unless upheld by God."[35]

What kept Carey going? Back in England, he had basked in vibrant congregational life. Now he was in a barren wasteland. He was isolated, discouraged, and dejected. He yearned for Spirit-wrought community like never before: "Felt much remains of dullness, and indisposition to the things of God. I see now the value of Christian society." Even when his spirits were lifted during times of happiness in family worship, Carey would still "sorely feel the loss of those public opportunities which I had enjoyed in England" (March 1, 1794).[36] Put simply, he longed for a church.

William Carey was a church-centered missionary. Historian Luke Waite observes, "From the streets of England to the bazaars of India, Carey was never far from the local church."[37]

---

34 Carter, *Journal and Selected Letters*, 24.

35 Carter, *Journal and Selected Letters*, 25.

36 Carter, *Journal and Selected Letters*, 18, 20.

37 Luke Waite, *May I Again Taste the Sweets of Social Religion* (Eugene, OR: Pickwick, 2023), xviii.

## CHURCH AS THE GOAL OF MISSIONS

Regardless of context, Carey always endeavored to practice biblical ecclesiology. This is why one of his first objectives was the formation of a church. Notice the aim of his heartfelt prayer from January 13, 1794: "O may I again taste the sweets of social religion which I have given up, and *see in this land of darkness a people formed for God*."[38]

Carey's prayer was answered. Two years later, he wrote to the Baptist Missionary Society: "A Baptist church is formed in this distant quarter of the globe."[39]

Far from hindering Carey's ministry, "Carey's devotion to the local church fueled his effectiveness in reaching the lost."[40] For one thing, it kept him in India. It served as a launchpad for gospel operations deeper into the country. It provided a model for future indigenous church leaders. Carey's ecclesiology propelled his missiology.

Today, too many well-intentioned cross-cultural workers have divorced ecclesiology from missiology. In doing so, they've departed from apostolic practice and the best examples of missions history. We've argued that church planting is the end-goal of all missions efforts. This is because, as Charles Bridges expressed it, "The church is the mirror, that reflects

38  Waite, *May I Again Taste*, 8. Emphasis added.
39  Waite, *May I Again Taste*, 33.
40  Waite, *May I Again Taste*, xix.

## CHAPTER 5

the whole effulgence of the Divine character. It is the grand scene, in which the perfections of Jehovah are displayed to the universe."[41]

So let's reconnect ecclesiology and missiology. After all, there's no mission without the church.

41 Charles Bridges, *The Christian Ministry* (1830; repr. Banner of Truth, 1980), 1.

6

# Churches Cooperating
# for Missions

Karl Gützlaff was a nineteenth-century pioneer missionary to China. By all accounts, he was a brilliant linguist who mastered Mandarin as well as Chinese culture. His tireless mobilization efforts led to new missionary societies in Europe, and many new missionaries joined his work. He said, "My love for China is inexpressible. I am burning for their salvation."[1] In China, his impressive language skills enabled him to be appointed as the Chinese secretary to the British governor of Hong Kong.

1 A. J. Broomhall, *Hudson Taylor and China's Open Century: Barbarians at the Gates* (London: Hodder and Stoughton, 1981), 184–85. Quoted in G. Wright Doyle, "Charles Gützlaff," Biographical Dictionary of Chinese Christianity website, accessed May 8, 2024, https://bdcconline.net/.

## CHAPTER 6

His gospel work, though, remained his greatest passion. But he insisted on directing it alone. In 1844, he founded the Chinese Union through which Christian literature could be distributed among the Chinese. Convinced that Chinese nationals would never listen to foreigners tell them the gospel, Gützlaff handpicked hundreds of national distributors he deemed "of good character" who could accomplish his distribution goals.[2] Every day, Gützlaff filled bags with New Testaments and gospel tracts. He instructed the distributors to hand out the literature while dozens of paid national evangelists explained the tracts to recipients. In addition to a monthly stipend, Gützlaff also covered the evangelists' travel expenses. In return, the evangelists submitted reports of their travels and, most importantly, results of their gospel witness. According to their reports, hundreds of nationals were being baptized every year!

On the strength of these impressive results, Gützlaff raised even more funds back in Europe. What Gützlaff didn't know was that it was all a sham. His team of handpicked evangelists and distributors were selling his literature back to the printer who then resold them to Gützlaff. Because no churches were established, there was no accountability. Because he had no

2  Doyle, "Charles Gützlaff."

**166**

### CHURCHES COOPERATING FOR MISSIONS

partners, there was no one to verify the results. Other missionaries were convinced that Gützlaff was being conned and tried to warn him.

But Gützlaff was stubborn. He would have none of it. He viewed missionaries as competitors. He accused them of being jealous of his results and prejudiced against the Chinese. He insisted that only he had firsthand knowledge of what was really happening. According to one historian, Gützlaff was "an insecure loner, sensitive and quick to perceive offense in relations with equals or those in authority."[3] By 1851, a heartbroken Gützlaff was unable to deny the truth any longer. He disbanded the Chinese Union.

Was Gützlaff a failure as a missionary? It's never that cut-and-dry. If you spend enough time around any missionaries, you'll find flaws in their approach, sin in their lives, and cracks in their character. There's much to admire in Gützlaff. He loved a spiritually starved people; he wanted them to know Christ. In fact, it's a bit ironic that Gützlaff was so connected as a mobilizer yet so alone as a missionary.

He teaches us all a valuable lesson: There's no reason to "go it alone" in missions. We all need accountability and help.

---

3   Jessie G. Lutz, *Opening China: Karl F. A. Gützlaff and Sino-Western Relations, 1827–1852*, Studies in the History of Christian Missions (Grand Rapids, MI: Eerdmans, 2008), 115. Quoted in Doyle, "Charles Gützlaff."

CHAPTER 6

If churches are the origin, the means, and the goal of missions, then missions works best when churches work together. This, too, is a part of God's design.

Since William Carey first left England, organizations that help facilitate partnership between churches have grown in popularity. Certainly many such organizations do wonderful work. And yet, churches should actively develop partnerships with other churches to share resources, educate pastors and missionaries, and share opportunities to declare the gospel to spiritually needy people.

In this chapter, we'll review some of the partnership we see among churches in the New Testament. Then we'll consider how churches can work together today in missions.

### New Testament Churches

In the Bible, local churches are independent but interdependent spiritual families. Each congregation has the responsibility and authority to make decisions concerning its own membership and leadership. And each church's elders have the responsibility and authority to lead their church in these kinds of decisions. This combination of elder leadership and congregational rule leads to maturity and growth (Eph. 4:11–16). Yet such independent churches should also be interdependent. Churches in the Bible helped each other

## CHURCHES COOPERATING FOR MISSIONS

regularly. Being variously gifted, they shared their resources with each other. Though geographically separated, they were united in the gospel. They were ambassadors and embassies of one kingdom, and they acted like it.

For instance, the church in Jerusalem initiated a famous partnership when a new church began among the Gentiles in Antioch. Jerusalem sent Barnabas, one of their most faithful leaders, to establish the new congregation (Acts 11:19–26). The Antioch church, prompted by the prophecy of a great famine, sent aid to their brothers in Judea (11:27–30). Good things happen when churches partner together.

The apostle Paul witnessed this partnership firsthand. Perhaps it prompted him to teach new churches to pray for one another and provide for one another. Perhaps that's why he organized the churches in Macedonia and Achaia to follow suit (Rom. 15:26–27).

Paul championed cooperation. He saw how churches can cooperate not only for mutual aid but also for missions. In Romans 15:23–24 he says, "But now, since I no longer have any room for work in these regions, and since I have longed for many years to come to you, I hope to see you in passing as I go to Spain, and to be helped on my journey there by you, once I have enjoyed your company for a while." Paul had a great desire to preach the gospel in Spain. But he knew he

## CHAPTER 6

needed help! So he hoped to receive encouraging fellowship and practical support for his journey through a partnership with the churches and Christians in Rome.

Similarly, the apostle John wrote his third epistle to encourage Christian cooperation. First, he tells his readers what they *should* do: cooperate in generous support of Christian ministers. He says, "We ought to support people like these, that we may be fellow workers for the truth" (3 John 8).

Second, he tells his readers what they *shouldn't* do: Don't follow Diotrephes's example. In sharp contrast to gospel ministers who gave their lives so others could hear the gospel, Diotrephes sought his own place. He refused to acknowledge the authority of the apostles. He was a loner.

Cooperation and partnership fill the pages of the New Testament. Churches shared love and greetings (Eph. 1:15). They shared good preachers (2 Cor. 8:18) and missionaries (3 John 5–6). They shared financial resources (1 Cor. 16:1–3). They prayed regularly for each other, and they thanked God when those prayers were answered (2 Cor. 9:12; Eph. 6:18). They imitated each other in Christian living (1 Thess. 2:14).[4]

Churches in the New Testament also worked together in missions. The churches in Antioch and Jerusalem supported

4  Jonathan Leeman, *One Assembly: Rethinking the Multisite and Multiservice Church Models*, 9Marks website (Wheaton, IL: Crossway, 2020), 105.

## CHURCHES COOPERATING FOR MISSIONS

Paul and Barnabas in their travels (Acts 11; 13; 15). The church in Derbe sent Paul and Barnabas back to Lystra, Iconium, and Antioch to appoint elders in those churches (14:21–23). Phil Newton explains: "Churches networking together, sending out leaders for strategic ministry with Paul, gave a pattern for unified church mission in post-apostolic days. This same pattern can be noted in the epistles of Ignatius a generation or more later. It's a good plan for our day as well."[5]

What can churches today learn from these examples?

### Churches Today

Recently, my (Scott's) church in Central Asia was greatly encouraged by a group of pastors from a dozen different Chinese churches in the United States who visited our city. These pastors strongly desire to join others in proclaiming Christ where his fame is not yet known. They said, "We are really good at ministering to Chinese people and working with Chinese Christians. But we want to proclaim Christ to all the nations." They came to listen and asked many questions. Mostly, they asked whether they could partner with our church by joining us to make disciples in our city. Although

5   Phil Newton, *The Mentoring Church: How Pastors and Congregations Cultivate Leaders* (Grand Rapids, MI: Kregel, 2017), 61.

## CHAPTER 6

there are very few churches in our city, they don't want to start a work that's disconnected from the churches already here. So here's the plan: They're sending mature Chinese believers to become members of our church, so they can increase the footprint of Christians in our city and seek out fresh opportunities for ministry.

When I was a missions pastor in the US, Ethiopian-American members of my church desired to do gospel work in Ethiopia. To aid them as best I could, I contacted our trusted partners in neighboring countries in East Africa. Working with those churches, we sent a small team of American and African pastors to Ethiopia's capital, Addis Ababa. Our goal was simple: to discern the status of churches in the city and ask what opportunities existed for outreach and missions there. To truly work well in Ethiopia, we needed to find a healthy church on the ground.

Eventually another church partner in the UAE connected us with an Ethiopian brother who had recently completed his pastoral internship. He had returned to Ethiopia and wanted to plant a church, so our team naturally decided to get behind him. This was a group that only God could have put together: American, Kenyan, and Ethiopian pastors working to discover good avenues for missions and ministry in Ethiopia.

As churches evaluate missionary candidates, partnerships should play a key part of the equation. Some candidates will be ready to start a new church among an unreached language group. Even in situations like these, they should go with as many other Christians as possible to form a church.

In church-centered missions, missionary care is a church-to-church endeavor. So if you're planning to send missionaries overseas, make sure you have a plan for church once they get there. In many cases, there will be a receiving church on the ground. But sometimes, those missionaries will be forming a church when they arrive with whoever came with them. This may seem like a small concern, but it's vital, and perhaps even more important than which agency you choose.

## The Delicate Dance of Missions

After attending seminary, Joe and Alyssa Miller were sent by Crossroads Church to serve in Baku, Azerbaijan, a gospel-needy Muslim city. Baku had a small but healthy church full of expats. Baku Baptist Church (BBC) could serve as the Millers' church home while they learned the language. Working with their pastoral staff at Crossroads, they decided to partner with Pioneering Sending (PS). The Millers served in Baku under their team leader, Steve, and his family, alongside

## CHAPTER 6

two other families. Steve helped them move in and became their language coach.

During their first few months in Baku, the Millers settled into the rhythm of their new life. They learned to buy groceries and navigate their neighborhood. They met with their PS team every week. They listened intently as Steve directed them in team meetings. He'd lived in the city for more than a decade, so they felt comfortable bringing their questions to him. They also enjoyed worshiping each Sunday at BBC. None of their teammates attended church with them, which they thought was a little strange, and after a couple of months they decided to join the church as members. Once a month, they had a video call with pastors from Crossroads.

The initial excitement of their new situation wore off quickly. Their life slid into a steady grind. Language learning was hard. After about a year, the Crossroads pastors noticed their fatigue and were concerned. They asked Joe and Alyssa probing questions; they wanted to figure out what was wrong so they could get them back "on track."

During their weekly team meetings, Steve also asked about their well-being and continued to direct their day-to-day activities. He said, "What you're experiencing is normal. More than anything else, you need to keep at it. Don't let up, just push through!"

The Millers were discouraged by this advice—and slightly frustrated, truth be told. Why would Steve maintain their language requirements? Why did he keep pressing them when they were clearly exhausted?

During their monthly video calls, the Crossroads pastors noticed the Millers' frustrations over Steve's leadership. They also couldn't decipher his logic, but they hoped for the best and sought to help Joe and Alyssa improve their relationship with Steve. Meanwhile, the Millers' church members at BBC also wanted to care for them. They prayed for them and offered their own input.

The Millers were receiving well-meaning, loving counsel from many sources—their sending agency, their sending church at home, and their local church on the field. But their advice often contradicted each other.

This is a fictional case study, but it's composed of real-life elements I have witnessed dozens of times. Missionaries end up receiving conflicting advice, especially when they're struggling.

One circumstance that complicates lines of authority is financial support. Many missionaries receive financial support from their supporters, from their missions agency, and even from their sending church. When financial support is involved, this will necessarily include a bit of managerial

## CHAPTER 6

authority.[6] Those with managerial authority over the missionary—often including their missions agency team, their field supervisor, their sending church, and sometimes other key financial supporters—do well when they don't overreach. Specifically, they should yield to the authority of the field-side church and their elders.

As we noted in chapter 4, the division of responsibility looks like this:

1. Sending churches invest precious resources. They send the missionaries and often commit significant financial resources to support them. As a result, they understandably expect to exercise some measure of *managerial authority* because these are "their" missionaries.

2. Overseas churches—in this case, BBC—accept missionaries into membership and regularly care for them. They exercise *pastoral authority*, but they also exercise a binding-and-loosing *ecclesial authority*. They formally affirm them as believers in the covenant of church membership and can discipline them if neces-

---

6   For more on managerial authority, see Jonathan Leeman, "The Manager (Command)," chap. 15 in *Authority: How Godly Rule Protects the Vulnerable, Strengthens Communities, and Promotes Human Flourishing* (Wheaton, IL: Crossway, 2023).

sary. Overseas churches do all this because these are "their" church members.

3. Missions agencies officially register missionaries as employees and also invest financial and personnel resources to support the team they join. Agencies usually develop a supporting network of member care, financial advisors, training personnel, and more to make sure missionaries can flourish. Missions agencies exercise *managerial authority* because these are "their" missionary employees.

As partners increase, the potential for conflict increases. To make it even trickier, these three kinds of authority often overlap. In extreme cases, we've seen desperately stressed-out missionaries use these scenarios to pit partners against each other. More commonly, we've seen missionaries get frustrated and exhausted by the constant contrary directions. That's why it's vital for these various partners to recognize and act within the boundaries of the authority they have by virtue of their roles.

The scenario above illustrates how important it is that sending churches continue to play an important role. They naturally function as wise counselors for the missionaries they send. But they should relinquish their missionaries as church members to whatever body they gather with overseas.

CHAPTER 6

## What Does Partnership Look Like?

### *An Oasis in the Desert*

Gavin Watson was a member of the Evangelical Christian Church of Dubai (ECCD) and a trusted attorney for the ruler of Ras Al Khaima (RAK), the northernmost emirate of the UAE. Through that relationship, this Arab sheikh generously granted land for ECCD to build a church in his domain. When ECCD's leaders received this amazing opportunity, they reached out to their partners throughout the world, including Capitol Hill Baptist Church in Washington, DC (CHBC), which had sent the Folmars to Dubai seven years earlier. Josh Manley, an elder of Third Avenue Baptist Church in Louisville, Kentucky, had been trained at CHBC and agreed to move with his family to RAK. He planted the church and raised support for a building that would become a strategic gospel outpost in a needy part of the world.

Because Josh had been qualified for missionary and pastoral service by these churches, he and his family were able to land in the UAE with support from an entire network of churches. Ten years of faithful service later, this church is an oasis for the gospel in a spiritual desert. Many believers have built friendships with the underreached local Emiratis. The church has been salt and light for the community. Some members

178

work in high government positions; others teach local high school students. For several years, at Christmastime dozens of nationals would visit the Manleys' house for an officially sponsored "cultural exchange event" and hear the true message of Christmas. Over the years, many people from different religious backgrounds have heard the gospel and come to Christ.

Because of the partnership among multiple churches in the US and the UAE, one church became a launchpad for gospel work in Arabia and beyond.

## *Help for Gospel Renegades*

For more than a decade, Josh Manley has trained and partnered with Afghan pastors who eventually led house churches in their home country. When Taliban forces overran Afghanistan in 2021, those pastors were on the run. One house church leader sent Josh a photo of the small room he was hiding in with his family, He texted him, "This is where I am living. We are hidden right now in different areas."[7] *World* magazine reported that the Taliban had contacted several of the pastors and warned, "We are coming for you."[8]

7   Josh Manley, "Afghan Pastors Ask for Prayer," 9Marks website, August 16, 2021, https://www.9marks.org/.
8   Emma Fowle, "What the Taliban Takeover Means for Afghanistan's Christians," *Premier Christianity* website, September 27, 2021, https://www.premierchristianity.com/.

## CHAPTER 6

Before they were in ministry in the Middle East, Josh and his wife, Jenny, worked in government. They leaned on their political contacts in Washington, DC, and spearheaded efforts to protect and support their friends. Jenny recalled, "We stayed up 24 hours and called people in DC, called people that work for the US government—I mean, everybody we could. . . . We were trying to connect all these people."[9] Missions agencies in the US had pulled their workers out of Afghanistan. Many ended up in the UAE. The Manleys counseled them as they processed grief and confusion.

But their friends were still stuck. The political and logistical hurdles were enormous. And yet, one Afghan leader told Josh, "Our hope is not in politics but in Jesus who is the King."

Against all odds, many Afghan leaders evacuated and found safe passage to the US, where they joined with local churches and began the recovery process. Sarah Zylstra reported, "The Afghan House Church leaders are now scattered across a handful of countries. But they're still connected, and they're still writing and podcasting good theology, now with much more freedom."[10] One of the leaders has built a 9Marks web page in Dari. Some have sought seminary training and remain

9   Sarah Zylstra, "Escape from Kabul," The Gospel Coalition, April 30, 2022, https://www.thegospelcoalition.org/.

10  Zylstra, "Escape from Kabul."

actively involved in strategic gospel work in Afghanistan, where the house churches continue to meet.

## *Ministry Multiplication*

As we saw in chapter 3, healthy churches overseas are platforms for ministry training and gospel influence. Pastoral training programs can become powerful resources for starting churches all around the world.

For example, McLean Bible Church (MBC) partners with several overseas churches like John's to fund their pastoral training programs. Through ECCD's pastoral training program, Christians from different countries are trained to become solid elders. Some of them stay at ECCD, but most return to their home countries and start new churches.

In one instance, a new national church was started in Nepal. Through our partnership with ECCD, MBC formed a new partnership with this new church. Our congregation offered critical support during their first years. Now, years later, that Nepali church has begun its own internship program and has spearheaded publishing work in the Nepali language. Don't miss this: This new church in Nepal was nobody's plan. The only plan was to commit to making ECCD a healthy church and to train pastors for ministry. And yet, through their faithfulness, God founded a new congregation

## CHAPTER 6

and, through committed partnership, churches in America played a helpful role.

### *Connecting Gospel Nomads*

When I (Scott) was a missions pastor in the US, a young woman from our congregation, Rachel, contacted me: "My company has assigned me to work in India! How can I leverage my job for the gospel?" I immediately texted Joseph, a trusted pastor in India. "Do you know of any faithful pastors or churches in her new city?" Without hesitating, he sent me the name and email address for Samuel. I wrote Samuel, and we spoke at length.

By God's grace, within just a few days of learning about her move, I connected Rachel with Samuel, though I'd never even heard of that city before. We visited Rachel after she'd been in her country for a year. On that trip we received glowing reviews. Samuel loved having Rachel as a member, and Rachel loved being a member. She even requested an extension of her assignment so she could keep serving her church.

### *Leveraging Networks in India*

I once arranged a team of elders and pastors from MBC to travel with me to India. Our goal was simple: Visit a retreat to meet new pastors and see how our church could encourage them in their work. National pastors retreats are great opportunities to develop partnerships.

My Indian pastor friend, Joseph, organized the retreat. I'd known Joseph for years, so I had lofty expectations for this trip. A year earlier, he'd told me, "Come and see: There are many faithful pastors and churches in India you can partner with."

The trip far exceeded our expectations. The first morning, we were all suffering from jet lag and woke up later than the Indian pastors. They started without us. While we slowly woke ourselves up with cold showers and coffee, seventy-five pastors had been standing outside in the cold for about an hour. Aligned in a circle, they listened intently as one pastor stood on a stump and preached to the group for about ten minutes. After his sermon, the other pastors then encouraged him and offered feedback on how to improve. They listened to two or three sermons each morning.

These faithful men represented churches throughout India. Neither the time of day nor the cold made a difference. They rose early to help one another become more faithful handlers of God's word. Some were serving in India's most difficult areas. Others were making plans to do the same. Our partnerships grew. And we were humbled at the privilege of supporting them.

CHAPTER 6

### *Partnering for Theological Education*

I met Timothy from Portugal through a mutual pastor friend. Timothy told me about his plan to start a new church in his gospel-starved country. I love supporting faithful national pastors. I passed his support needs to the review team at MBC, and they agreed to begin a formal partnership with Timothy and his new church.

Within two years of moving to Portugal, he started a theological seminary. As far as we knew, this would be one of the only biblically faithful evangelical seminaries in the country. Through another partnership, our church was able to provide a shipping container full of textbooks and reference materials at the cost of the shipping alone. We were able to do the same with other international seminaries too.

### *Partners in Persecution*

Suleiman was being hunted. Originally from the island of Zanzibar, he had completed his pastoral training in the UAE and returned home. He'd begun preaching Christ to his former Muslim friends. When several came to faith in Christ, there was a violent backlash.

Suleiman's family disowned him. He tried to return to Dubai but was forcibly removed from an airplane by police and interrogated three times. Authorities threatened to rape and imprison him if he wouldn't renounce Christ. They pressured him to give video testimony and spread lies about Christianity.

In response, Suleiman wrote a three-page "confession" for the police. It was filled with Bible verses that explained the gospel. The authorities were at a loss. They didn't know what to do, so they simply released him and ordered him to keep quiet.

Life didn't get easier for Suleiman. He and the new disciples received anonymous death threats. One convert's house was burned; another convert was murdered. Still another was horribly raped and threatened. Suleiman fully expected that one day he would either be dead or doing church-planting in prison.

Somehow, he escaped to a nearby East African country. He was taken in and cared for by a church there. But Suleiman's enemies found him, and the church that helped him was also threatened. Anti-terrorism police were called in to provide protection.

Suleiman was experiencing Paul's prediction that "all who desire to live a godly life in Christ Jesus will be persecuted" (2 Tim. 3:12). But it wasn't only Suleiman who was caught up in the persecution. The Christians who were with him were in trouble too. Eventually, an entire network of churches got involved. Churches as far away as New Zealand and the United States sacrificially cared for the victims of the backlash.

CHAPTER 6

Here's a question: Why? Why were congregations in East Africa, Dubai, New Zealand, and the United States so eager to help a Zanzibari Muslim convert, even when it posed a risk to themselves? Perhaps it was because, as Paul said, "If one member suffers, all suffer together" (1 Cor. 12:26). They cared for their brother because they were members of the same universal body. Thanks to this joint effort, Suleiman and the rape victim are now married and safely in another location. They're pursuing training for future ministry.

These partnership examples display the same spirit of cooperation and partnership that fills the pages of the New Testament. These churches love one another (Eph. 1:15). They share good preachers (2 Cor. 8:18) and missionaries (3 John 5–6). They help each other with physical needs (1 Cor. 16:1–3). They pray regularly for each other (2 Cor. 9:12; Eph. 6:18) and imitate each other in Christian living (1 Thess. 2:14).

They do all this so that more churches can be started. Because missions is church centered.

Churches that actively develop partnerships aren't being innovative. They're illustrating the spirit of the New Testament. As we follow God's design, we'll continue to see God use cooperation to bring himself glory among the nations. Missions works best when churches work together.

# Conclusion

A seasoned veteran missionary sat at lunch with a young, troubled couple. The couple had been on the field for a while but, by their own admission, they were "spiritually dried up." They hadn't been to church in three years. Their team leader considered Sunday morning team meetings their church, but he sometimes invited non-Protestants to teach the Bible. There were no elders, no ordinances, and no community. The couple had been told there were no healthy churches in the area. When the husband pushed back, he got permission to explore the church scene. To his surprise, he found a couple healthy ones nearby.

The veteran recalled, "He told me all this in a hushed voice like he was almost scared people were going to hear this. I just sat there listening and thinking, 'This poor guy!' This is the reality of where we are."

Sadly, this is the reality of where we've been for more than a generation. Weak ecclesiology on the mission field is nothing

## CONCLUSION

new. Another veteran missionary observed, "In spite of all the talk about church planting . . . the church remains an anomaly for most missionaries. At times it's a useful tool and handy source of personnel, material, and money. At others it's an uneducated and lethargic group which insists on getting in the way and slowing up the whole program of world missions."[1] That was written in 1972.

Bad ecclesiology still leads to bad missions. Among the first to suffer the consequences are the missionaries themselves. Their discipleship falters, their marriages strain, their evangelism weakens, and their tenures are cut short. "Free agent" missionaries don't last long.

Bad ecclesiology harms missionaries, but it also harms the people they're trying to reach. A team of missionaries was meeting with Muslim-background believers in a cosmopolitan Arabian city. The gathering was a fellowship of sorts, but not a church. The former Muslims professed Christ, but they had no elder oversight; they did not observe the Lord's Supper; and they weren't subject to the accountability of a congregation. Many of these young believers were struggling. One Palestinian woman was beset with loneliness and depression. Some of the leaders pointed her to the church for fellowship and care, but other missionaries were skeptical of church involvement,

---

1   Personal correspondence from Leon Blosser to Stanley Line, June 17, 1972.

## CONCLUSION

whether Arabic or English-speaking (she spoke both). They believed that the presence of "Christian-background" people would taint an indigenous expression of faith.

In the end, a Saudi believer finally persuaded the Palestinian woman to join a church. The Saudi said, "I've been reading my Bible and learning how much it talks about church. You need to come with me to church—that will help you." And so she did. It took the *Saudi* believer telling the *Palestinian* believer about the church. Most of the Western missionaries stayed silent.

It doesn't have to be that way. Hassan, a Somali living in Saudi Arabia, was converted through gospel teaching on the internet. Missionaries in Saudi met him and learned he was a believer. They invited Hassan to attend their house-church, but he kept his distance, instead attending "online ministry" for support and guidance. But after his brother threatened to kill him for his faith, Hassan was shaken. The missionaries counseled him and again encouraged church attendance for his support and growth. This time Hassan agreed. When he experienced in-person, life-on-life community, teaching, and singing in the church, including the baptism of a Saudi believer, Hassan concluded, "If I had known what it was like to meet in person, I never would have met online." He's still committed to that church.

In this book we have argued that churches are the Bible's missions strategy—the origin, the means, and the goal of

## CONCLUSION

missions. In doing so, we stand in a long line of those who went before. John Paton, who devoted thirty years to preaching the gospel to cannibals in the South Sea islands, gave this closing counsel to missionaries:

> Plant down your forces in the heart of one Tribe or Race, where the same language is spoken. Work solidly from that centre, building up with patient teaching and life-long care *a Church* that will endure. Rest not till every People and Language and Nation has such a Christ-centre throbbing in its midst, with the pulses of the New Life at full play.[2]

Paton's advice is different from the prevailing wisdom. Modern movement-driven missions downplays the unflashy, the ordinary, the slow—contrary to Jesus's prediction of kingdom growth: "First the blade, then the ear, then the full grain in the ear" (Mark 4:28). So, as Paton said: "Rush not from Land to Land, from People to People, in a breathless and fruitless mission. . . . The consecrated Common-sense that builds for Eternity will receive the fullest approval of God in Time."[3] The church is God's consecrated common sense—the origin, the means, and the goal of missions.

2 John G. Paton, *Missionary to the New Hebrides* (Edinburgh, UK: Banner of Truth, 1965), 496.

3 Paton, *Missionary to the New Hebrides*, 496. Emphasis added.

# General Index

*a cappella* singing, 50
Abrahamic covenant, 5, 35
accountability, 91, 123, 129, 166–67
Achaia, 169
adoption, 7
Advocates of Church Planting Movements, 13–14
"Affirmations and Denials Concerning World Mission," 12
Afghanistan, 128, 179, 180
Al Nahyan, Mohammed bin Zayed, 140
ambition, 95
Antioch, 3, 19, 69, 70, 88, 89, 96, 121, 169, 170, 171
Any-3, 118, 157
application, 12, 59
Arabic, 119–20
Arabs, 106, 111, 113, 188
Armenian Church, 115–16, 138

Ash, Christopher, 31–32
Australia, 101
authority, 40, 44, 122, 168
Azerbaijan, 173

Bahrain, 4, 5
Baku Baptist Church (BBC), 173, 174, 175
baptism, 43–47, 49, 55, 66, 72, 82, 99, 137
Baptist Missionary Society, 18, 160, 163
Barnabas, 69–70, 75, 88–89, 96, 121, 143, 171
barriers, 73–78
Basil of Caesarea, 131
Bavinck, J. H., 145
Berea, 89n4
"best practices" approach, 54
Bible, downplaying of, 11–15
Bible studies, 135

## GENERAL INDEX

biblical Christianity, 32, 129
biblical leadership, 51–54
"big tent" organization, 100
binding-and-loosing authority,
    121, 122, 176
Blosser, Leon, 110–13
Bolivia, 92, 93
Bonar, Andrew, 95n11
born again, 46
Botswana, 100
Bowers, Paul, 145
Brainerd, David, 156
"branded Christianity," 150, 151,
    152
Bridges, Charles, 163–64
"broad mission," 64
Buddhism, 31, 32, 37, 49
Buser, Brooks, 99

Caesarea, 3
Capitol Hill Baptist Church
    (Washington, DC), 90, 178
Carey, William, 4, 18–20,
    102n20, 160–63, 168
Caruthers, Ken, 50n38
cell, 26
Chantry, Walter, 11, 98–99, 110–12
character, 95–96
China, 155, 165–67
Chinese Union, 166, 167
Christian adherent, 76n10
Christian life, 7, 17, 25, 85–86,
    117, 135, 138
Christianity, as church shaped, 8

church
    authority of, 44
    corporate life of, 129–30
    definition of, 15–16, 23, 27, 99
    discipleship in, 133–36
    downplaying of, 8–11, 27, 47
    as gathering, 30–34
    and the gospel, 5
    health of, 123–25
    love in, 125–28
    as means and ends of missions,
        6, 20, 138
    peace in, 128–29
    as a people, 34–36
    as pillar and buttress of the
        truth, 54–55
    as pulling support, 108–9
    and salvation, 6–8
    service in, 130–32
    starting and strengthening of,
        69–71
    as a temple, 36–39
    what it does, 39–54
church covenant, 147–48
church discipline, 48, 176–77
church membership, 11, 48, 65,
    91, 120–21, 144, 153, 176–77
church planting, 64, 73, 99, 141,
    188
Church Planting Movements, 94,
    118, 150, 157–58
church-centered missions, 15–20
church-centered sending, 88–90
Churchill, Winston, 73

## GENERAL INDEX

Cilicia, 3
Clark, Elliot, 54n43, 109
Clifton Baptist Church, 106
Clow, W. M., 49
Clowney, Edmund, 36
Coleman, Doug, 33
Coles, David, 40n28
Colombia, 113
colonialist mindsets, 13, 26
compassion, 80
competence, 94–95
confession, 44
Congress for World Evangelization, 76
contextualization, 13, 26, 99, 155
conversion, 7, 11, 82, 85, 99, 132, 162
conviction, 94
cooperation, 169–70, 186
Corinth, 3, 109, 146
corporate evangelism, 38n24
corporate prayer, 135
Crete, 143
cultural barriers, 75, 78
cultural relativism, 12n11
culture, 36
Cyprus, 69

deacons, 52, 97
dentistry, 24
depression, 188
Derbe, 89n4, 171
Dever, Mark, 55
DeYoung, Kevin, 72

Diotrephes, 170
discernment, 108–9
disciple making, 64, 72, 91
Disciple Making Movements, 94, 118
discipleship, 8, 9, 14, 16–17, 63, 67, 83, 133–36, 150, 188
discipline, 48, 134–35, 176–77
Discovery Bible Studies, 40, 100
doctrinal minimalism, 10, 12, 109, 152–53
doctrine, 150, 151, 154
Dome of the Rock, 21, 37

ecclesial authority, 122, 176
ecclesiology, 9–10, 14, 27, 28, 94, 119, 163–64, 187–88
ecumenism, 115–16
Edwards, Jonathan, 156, 157
Egypt, 90
elders, 11, 52, 55, 97, 133, 143, 147, 160, 168, 187
encouragement, 106–7
entertainment, 41
Ephesus, 3, 146
equipping, 107
Ethiopia, 172
Ethiopian eunuch, 45n31
Evangelical Christian Church of Dubai (ECCD), 15, 89–90, 113, 178, 181
Evangelical Lutheran Church, 26
evangelicals, 76–77n10, 93, 116, 140–41

## GENERAL INDEX

evangelism, 25, 64, 72, 73, 80, 95, 102, 107, 133, 157
excommunication, 116
experts, 98
"export problem," 26
expositional preaching, 42–43, 90–91
extraordinary means, 14, 156

faithfulness, 132
false brothers, 109
false conversions, 28
false dichotomies, 153, 154, 155
false religion, 33
false teaching, 150
family, 125
Farah, Warrick, 151n19
fellowship, 26, 91, 134
female missionaries, 95
finances, 103, 105–6, 170, 175–76
foreign languages, 74
forgiveness, 63, 69, 126–27, 144
Four Fields, 94, 118
"free agent" missionaries, 188
friendship, 37–38
fulfillment, 61
Fuller, Andrew, 19

Galilee, 69
garden of Eden, 35
Garner, David, 32
gathering, 30–34
generosity, 105–6, 131
Gentiles, 75, 144, 169

geographic barriers, 75, 78
Germany, 101
gifts, 102
Gilbert, Greg, 72
globalization, 20
God
  doctrine of, 94
  dwelling of, 37
  glory of, 17, 23, 35, 91–92, 138, 141, 142
  sovereignty of, 158
good works, 64, 71–72, 154
Goodell, William, 115, 117
gospel
  as audible and visible, 23
  and churches, 5
  and doctrine, 151
  power of, 128
  preaching of, 3
  proclamation of, 137, 143
  urgency of, 68
  worldwide purposes of, 91
gospel friendship, 38
Grace Baptist Church (Carlisle, PA), 110, 113
Great Commission, 10, 15, 29, 30, 43, 44, 47, 49, 51, 55, 58–59, 60n1, 63, 66, 77, 85, 134, 141, 143, 151, 153
Great Constitution, 30
"group decisions," 46
guilt, 95
Gützlaff, Karl, 165–67

## GENERAL INDEX

Harvey Lane Baptist Church, 18
Hawthorne, Steven, 148
healthy church, 123–25, 152–53
heresy, 150
Hinduism, 74, 101, 150n16
Hindus, 4, 19, 31, 32, 45, 104
Hirsh, Alan, 151n19
Holy Spirit
  commissioning of, 70, 96
  empowerment of, 63
  guidance from, 16
  new birth from, 129
  supernatural demonstrations of, 74, 158
horizontal reconciliation, 7
hospitality, 50n38, 108, 113

Iconium, 3, 171
idealism, 95, 116
Illyricum, 79
imprisonment, 34
India, 4, 18, 46, 74–75, 90, 101, 103, 149, 150, 155, 161, 182, 183
indigenous leadership, 48
individualism, 8, 85–86
indoctrination, 151–52
Indonesia, 90
Insider Movement (IM), 32, 94, 118
intellectual assent, 154
International Mission Board, 15, 157–58
Iraq, 4, 128
Islam, 32, 35

Japan, 90
Jerusalem, 21–22, 169, 170
Jesus Christ
  blood of, 7
  death and resurrection of, 35, 45, 62
  divinity of, 86
  exclusivity of, 94
  greatness of, 51
  as head of the church, 52, 88
  on missions, 60–61
Johnson, Andy, 89, 96n13, 104
Jordan, 90
Joshua Project, 76–77
Judea, 69, 73
Julian, 131

Kabbalah, 37
Kabwata Baptist Church, 100, 113
Kathmandu, 101
Kazakhstan, 90, 101
Kebreab, S., 157n28
Kennedy, Burwell, 140
Kennedy, Marian, 140
Koine Greek, 75
Kuwait, 43

language barriers, 73–74, 78
language learning, 82, 95–96, 99, 124
leadership, 51–54
Leeman, Jonathan, 26, 44n30
Libya, 90
Livingstone, David, 158–59

## GENERAL INDEX

local church, 30, 31, 39, 87–88, 104, 119, 121, 123, 162
loneliness, 188
Lord's Supper, 47–49, 55, 160, 188
love, 125–28
Lull, Raymond, 75–76
Lystra, 3, 171

Macedonia, 75, 169
McGavran, Donald, 38, 46, 148–49
McLean Bible Church (MBC), 15, 181, 182, 184
Malawi, 100
man-centered ecclesiology, 28
managerial authority, 122, 175–76, 177
Manley, Jenny, 180
Manley, Josh, 178–79, 180
marriage, 8, 92
Martyn, Henry, 74–75, 120
maturity, 154
Mbewe, Conrad, 38–39n26, 106, 141, 144
M'Cheyne, Robert Murray, 95
means, of missions, 16–17
means of grace, 14, 123, 148
membership, 11, 48, 65, 91, 120–21, 144, 153, 176–77
methodology, 118, 119
Miller, Alyssa, 173–75
Miller, Joe, 173–75
minimalism, 10, 12, 109, 152–53

missiology, 9–10, 15, 47, 64, 151n19, 163–64
mission, 64
missionaries
  assessing of, 93–96
  and baptism, 46
  as Christians, 92–93
  definition of, 64
  and local church, 5, 8–10, 39
  support of, 105–6, 173
  visitation of, 57–58
missions
  as across barriers, 73–78
  as church-centered, 15–20
  definition of, 16, 59–60, 64–65
  and evangelism, 142–43
  and good works, 71–72
  ultimate end of, 17
missions agencies, 8, 10, 11, 12n12, 55, 66, 81, 88, 95, 97–100, 173, 175–76, 177, 180
missions committees, 96n13
missions methodology, 118, 119
moralism, 147
Morocco, 90, 103
Mounce, William, 53n42
Mount of Olives, 21
Mount Sinai, 23, 35
movement-driven missions, 13, 25n7, 26, 38, 52, 54, 149–50, 156, 190

## GENERAL INDEX

multiplication, 3, 97, 109, 156, 181–82

Muslims, 4, 9, 21, 25, 31, 32, 40, 42, 49, 86n1, 87, 99, 104, 108, 117–18, 126, 129, 130, 184, 188

Namibia, 100
Native Americans, 156
needs, 81
neglect, 10
Nepal, 90, 181
new birth, 29, 129
New Guinea, 113
New Testament
  churches of, 168–71
  gospel spread in, 18
  local church in, 88–89
  missions in, 71
  persecution in, 34
New Zealand, 185–86
Newton, Phil, 171
Niger, 95, 159–60
Nigeria, 100, 113
nominal Christianity, 47
nonbelievers, 54n43, 125, 126, 128, 129, 133

Oasis Mission Hospital, 110, 139, 140
obedience, 154
obedience-based discipleship, 100
Old Testament, 62
Oman, 4

"one another" commands, 83, 120–21
online ministry, 189
ordinances, 11, 48, 160, 187
ordinary churchmanship, 65
ordinary means of grace, 14–15, 123
origin, of missions, 16
Orthodox Church, 115–16
overseas visits, 107
overseers, 52

Papua New Guinea, 1, 136
parachurch agencies, 5, 11, 16, 55, 98n15
parenting, 8, 52
partnership, 98, 107, 168, 170, 173, 177, 186
Passover, 47
pastoral authority, 122, 123, 176
pastors, 52, 135
Paton, John, 190
Paul
  and Antioch church, 88–89, 121
  on churches, 143–46
  on cooperation, 169–70
  as persecutor, 69
  preaching of, 43
  priorities of, 79
  second journey of, 19, 70
peace, 128–29
Pentecost, 69, 73, 144
people, 34–36
people groups, 76

## GENERAL INDEX

"People Movements," 38, 149
persecution, 3, 34, 45, 51, 69, 116–17, 137, 184–86
Person of Peace, 100, 118
Perspectives, 148–49
philosophical differences, 105–6
Phoenicia, 69
Pioneering Sending (PS), 173–74
Piper, John, 142
Pisidian Antioch, 3
polytheism, 45
poor, 71–72, 130, 132
pragmatism, 10, 28, 109, 158
Pratt, Zane, 158
prayer, 106–7, 112
preaching, 3, 23, 39–43, 90–91, 147
primary doctrines, 152
profession of faith, 46, 47, 121
prosperity gospel, 147
psychology, 13
Puerto Rico, 113
pulling support, 108–9

*qahal*, 31
qualifications, 65–68, 69, 71, 88, 92, 160
Qur'an, 118

Radius International, 99
receiving church, 41, 173
"recent convert" prohibition, 53
reconciliation, 7
Red Crescent, 16

regulative discipline, 135
repentance, 62–63, 69, 134
responsibility, 176
restorative discipline, 134–35
resurrection, 62
revivals, 13, 156–57, 158
Rhodes, Matt, 86n1, 98
Ring, David, 78–79
Roman Catholic Church, 26
Roman Empire, 75
Russia, 47
Rwanda, 100

salvation, 6–8, 86
Samaria, 69
Saudi Arabia, 50
Scripture
  authority of, 40
  inerrancy of, 94
  missions in, 60–63
  translation of, 74–75
secondary doctrines, 152
seminary, 8, 42, 58, 81, 117–18, 152, 180, 184
sending agency, 97–100
sending church, 8, 41, 122, 136–37, 176
service, 130–32
service projects, 72
sexual immorality, 133–34
Shipman, Mike, 157
sickness, 112, 132
"sideways energy," 146–48
Sierra Leone, 100

## GENERAL INDEX

Silas, 70
simplistic definitions, 78
Sinai covenant, 35
singing, 49–51, 55, 97
"slow to grow approach," 14, 148
social commentary, 41
Solomon, 36
Southgate Fellowship, 12, 17, 88, 121–22
spiritual growth, 123
statement of faith, 86, 94, 147
Steller, Tom, 104–5
Stiles, Mack, 28
straw man arguments, 150–55
submission, 129
substitutionary death, 62
success, 118
suffering, 34, 80, 130
support, 105–6
syncretism, 47, 150
Syria, 3

Taliban, 179
Tanzania, 100
tattoos, 147
teaching, 39–43, 143
temple, 36–39
Tennent, Timothy C., 60n1
tentmakers, 87, 106
testimonies, 6–7
theological education, 80, 184
theological minimalism, 10, 12, 109, 152–53
theological misalignment, 99

theology, 11–15, 149
Thessalonica, 89n4
Third Avenue Baptist Church (Louisville, KY), 178
Titus, 143
"top-down" organization, 100
traditionalism, 155
Training for Trainers (T4T), 52–53, 118
Trinity, 94
Troas, 3
truth, 54–55
Turkey, 50n38, 128, 131–32

unbelievers, 54n43, 125, 128, 129, 133
"underground" church, 33–34
UNICEF, 16
union with Christ, 45
Union Church of Istanbul, Turkey, 15
United Arab Emirates (UAE), 15, 24n3, 29, 90, 101, 110, 139–41, 172, 180
United States, 185–86
unity, 38n24, 97, 128
Universal Disciple, 118
unreached peoples, 76, 137
Uzbekistan, 108

Van Ess, Dorothy, 24n3
Van Ess, John, 24n3
vertical reconciliation, 7
visitation, 57–58, 81, 107

## GENERAL INDEX

Waite, Luke, 162
Watson, David, 25n7, 28, 40,
    53–54, 150–51, 157
Watson, Gavin, 178
Watson, Paul, 25n7, 28, 40,
    53–54, 150–51, 157
Watts, Isaac, 156–57
Wesley, John, 93
Western Christianity, 2, 26, 32,
    42
Western culture, 49
Western Wall, 22, 37
Winter, Ralph, 148
word of God, 43, 61

World Evangelical Alliance, 135
worship, 23, 49–51, 91–92, 124,
    142

Yembiyembi language, 2

Zambia, 100
Zanzibar, 184
Zimbabwe, 100
Zoroastrianism, 37
Zuckerberg, Mark, 155
Zwemer, Amy, 5
Zwemer, Samuel, 4, 20, 24–25,
    33, 112
Zylstra, Sarah, 180

# Scripture Index

*Genesis*
4:8............. 127

*Exodus*
15:1 ........... 50

*Leviticus*
26:12.......... 35

*Deuteronomy*
4:10 .......... 31

*Judges*
21:25.......... 28
22.............. 24, 28

*1 Kings*
8:27 .......... 36

*Nehemiah*
8:8............. 42

*Psalms*
book of........ 61

96:3 ........... 92
100:1.......... 50

*Ecclesiastes*
4:8............. 127
12:12.......... 118

*Isaiah*
66.............. 137
66:18–19 ..... 137

*Matthew*
book of........ 44
5:14 .......... 142
16.............. 44, 44n30
16:17–19 ..... 30
16:18.......... 2, 30, 35
18.............. 44, 44n30
18:18.......... 44, 121
18:20.......... 133
24:14.......... 3, 59
28.............. 44, 44n30
28:18–20 ..... 30, 59, 60n1, 63

## SCRIPTURE INDEX

28:19 . . . . . . . . . . 23, 47, 77
28:20 . . . . . . . . . . 14, 134, 152

*Mark*
4:28 . . . . . . . . . . 158, 190
8:38 . . . . . . . . . . 33
16:14–18 . . . . . 60n1

*Luke*
4:21 . . . . . . . . . . 43
8:15 . . . . . . . . . . 158
14:12–14 . . . . . 130
17:4 . . . . . . . . . . 127
21:33 . . . . . . . . . . 61
22:19 . . . . . . . . . . 47
24:24 . . . . . . . . . . 62
24:33 . . . . . . . . . . 60
24:44–47 . . . . . 60
24:44–49 . . . . 60n1, 61
24:46–47 . . . . . 62
24:49 . . . . . . . . . . 63

*John*
2:19 . . . . . . . . . . 36
13:34–35 . . . . . 125
16:2 . . . . . . . . . . 33
17:21 . . . . . . . . . . 38n24, 125
20:19–23 . . . . . 60n1
21:25 . . . . . . . . . . 51

*Acts*
book of . . . . . . . 3, 44, 60, 62
1:7 . . . . . . . . . . . 153
1:7–8 . . . . . . . . . . 60n1

1:8 . . . . . . . . . . . 60
2:11 . . . . . . . . . . 73
2:38 . . . . . . . . . . 45
2:41 . . . . . . . . . . 73, 144
2:42 . . . . . . . . . . 40, 45, 48
2:47 . . . . . . . . . . 3, 131
5:11 . . . . . . . . . . 69
5:12 . . . . . . . . . . 3n3
8 . . . . . . . . . . . . . 69
8:1 . . . . . . . . . . . 3
8:4 . . . . . . . . . . . 3
8:38 . . . . . . . . . . 45n31
9:31 . . . . . . . . . . 3, 69
11 . . . . . . . . . . . . x, 171
11:19–26 . . . . . 169
11:25 . . . . . . . . . . 70
11:26 . . . . . . . . . . 3n3, 69
11:27–30 . . . . . 169
13 . . . . . . . . . . . . x, 96, 171
13:2 . . . . . . . . . . 88
13:3 . . . . . . . . . . 89, 121
14:21 . . . . . . . . . . 3n3, 143
14:21–23 . . . . . x, 171
14:22–23 . . . . . 70
14:23 . . . . . . . . . . 53n42, 143
14:27 . . . . . . . . . . 106, 121
14:27–28 . . . . . 89
15 . . . . . . . . . . . . x, 171
15:35 . . . . . . . . . . 19, 89n4, 121
15:36 . . . . . . . . . . 70, 107
15:41 . . . . . . . . . . 3n3, 70
16:11 . . . . . . . . . . 19
17:2 . . . . . . . . . . 43

## SCRIPTURE INDEX

18:8 .......... 3n3
18:11.......... 41, 71, 146
18:22.......... 3n3, 89n4, 121
19:9 .......... 3n3
19:9–10....... 146
20:4 .......... 89n4
20:6 .......... 3n3
20:7 .......... 48
20:17.......... 3n3
26:18.......... 144
29.............. 28

*Romans*
1:16 .......... 156
6:2............. 45
6:3–4.......... 45
6:17 .......... 153
10:2 .......... 154
12:2 .......... 155
12:3 .......... 96
15:19.......... 144
15:19–20 ..... 79
15:23–24 ..... 79, 169
15:26–27 ..... 169
16:5 .......... 31
16:16.......... 18, 145

*1 Corinthians*
4:17 .......... 145
9:22 .......... 118
11:1 .......... 52, 91
11:26.......... 49
11:27.......... 48
12:26.......... 186

14:11.......... 73
15:3 .......... 153
16:1–3 ....... 170, 186

*2 Corinthians*
4:6............. 91
5:17–20....... 63
6:14 .......... 33
8:18 .......... x, 170, 186
8:19 .......... 18
8:23 .......... 89n4
9:12 .......... 170, 186
11:26.......... 109
13:11.......... 127

*Galatians*
1:6–9.......... 154
2:10 .......... 130

*Ephesians*
1:13 .......... 151
1:15 .......... 170, 186
2.............. 7
2:4............. 7
2:6............. 7
2:11–22....... ix
2:13 .......... 7
2:14–15....... 39
2:15–16....... 128
2:19 .......... 38
2:22 .......... 37
3:10 .......... 23, 142
4:11 .......... 54
4:11–16....... 168

203

## SCRIPTURE INDEX

5:8 ............ 142
5:18–19 ....... 50
6:18 .......... 18, 170, 186

*Colossians*
1:18 .......... 52
1:28 .......... 146
2:9 ............ 36
3:10 .......... 155

*1 Thessalonians*
2:14 .......... 170, 186
2:17–3:5 ...... 71
3:12–13 ....... 127

*2 Thessalonians*
1:4 ............ 145

*1 Timothy*
book of ....... 53n42, 113
3:1–13 ........ 95
3:2 ............ 52, 53n42, 152
3:6 ............ 53
3:8 ............ 52
3:15 .......... 55
4:11 .......... 41
5:22 .......... 52

*2 Timothy*
1:12 .......... 154
1:13 .......... 153
2:2 ............ 90
2:15 .......... 40, 152
3:12 .......... 185

*Titus*
book of ....... 53n42
1:5 ............ 143
1:9 ............ 52, 53n42, 152
2:1 ............ 41, 151
2:10 .......... 72, 126
3:13 .......... 105

*Hebrews*
book of ....... 23
3:13 .......... 135
10:24–25 ..... 65
10:25 ......... 31, 34, 121
10:33–34 ..... 34
12:22–23 ..... 22
12:23 ......... 30
13:1 .......... 121
13:13 ......... 34
13:17 ......... 121

*James*
1:27 .......... 130
2:26 .......... 154
3:1 ............ 152
4:1 ............ 127

*1 Peter*
2:4 ............ 34
2:5 ............ 37
2:9 ............ 34
2:10 .......... ix, 6, 35
2:11 .......... 34
3:8 ............ 127
5:3 ............ 52

## SCRIPTURE INDEX

*1 John*
3:14 .......... 127
3:17–18 ....... 131
4:1 ............. 109

*2 John*
10 ............. 109

*3 John*
5–6 ........... 170, 186
5–8 ........... x
6 ............... 89n4, 104
6–8 ........... 18

7 ............... 95, 104, 108
8 ............... 105, 170
9–10 .......... x

*Jude*
3 ............... 154
12 ............. 48

*Revelation*
book of ....... 142, 145
2:1 ............. 142
5:9 ............. 51

## Building Healthy Churches

9Marks exists to equip church leaders with a biblical vision and practical resources for displaying God's glory to the nations through healthy churches.

To that end, we want to see churches characterized by these nine marks of health:

1. Expositional Preaching
2. Gospel Doctrine
3. A Biblical Understanding of Conversion and Evangelism
4. Biblical Church Membership
5. Biblical Church Discipline
6. A Biblical Concern for Discipleship and Growth
7. Biblical Church Leadership
8. A Biblical Understanding of the Practice of Prayer
9. A Biblical Understanding and Practice of Missions

---

Find all our Crossway titles and other resources at 9Marks.org.

# 9Marks Church-Centered Missions Series

 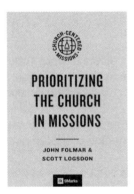

In the 9Marks Church-Centered Missions series, pastors and missionaries from around the world demonstrate the local church's God-given responsibility to train and send believers for missions work. Explaining how to work together to plant churches across significant geographical, cultural, or linguistic barriers, these books help readers recover a vision for the central role local churches should play in fulfilling the Great Commission.

For more information, visit **crossway.org**.